WE HAVE A CHOICE:

LET'S JUST DO IT

How the western worldview of progress has resulted in global inequality and threatens the health of the planet

A STUDY GUIDE FOR DISCUSSION GROUPS

Sharon Thompson

WE HAVE A CHOICE: LET'S JUST DO IT
How the western worldview of progress has resulted in global inequality and threatens the health of the planet
A STUDY GUIDE FOR DISCUSSION GROUPS
© 2020 Sharon Thompson

Published by Texianer Verlag
Johannesstraße 12
78609 Tuningen
Germany
www.texianer.com
for
The Hugh & Helene Schonfield
World Service Trust
www.schonfield.org
Study Edition
ISBN: 9783949197222

WE HAVE A CHOICE: LET'S JUST DO IT

This moment in history marks the end of a long, sad tale of greed and murder by the white races.

*Europeans and Americans have spent five centuries conquering, plundering, exploiting and polluting the earth **in the name of human progress.***

Chris Hedges

I refuse to accept the view that mankind is so tragically bound to the starless midnight of racism and war that the bright daybreak of peace and brotherhood can never become a reality…I believe that unarmed truth and unconditional love will have the final word.

Martin Luther King, Jr.

ABOUT THE AUTHOR

Sharon Thompson and her husband of sixty years, Gordon, a retired dairy farmer, are the parents of six daughters (and now six sons-in-law) who have blessed them with twenty grandchildren and nine great-grandchildren. Her family is her greatest love and joy. Her hope is that this study guide will play a role in advancing a worldwide discussion that will lead to a reclaimed world of love, peace, and justice for all people everywhere.

Table of Contents

ABOUT THE AUTHOR..5

INTRODUCTION..9

LESSON 1: DOMINATION – FROM LOCAL TO WORLD..13

LESSON 2: ECONOMIC GLOBALIZATION..27

LESSON 3: CAPITALISM AND CLIMATE CHANGE / SPECIES EXTINCTION........................39

LESSON 4: CORPORATIONS...53

LESSON 5: INTERNATIONAL CONTROL MECHANISMS...65

LESSON 6: DOMESTIC CONTROL MECHANISMS...79

LESSON 7: THE WESTERN WORLDVIEW AND HOW IT IS SUSTAINED...............................91

LESSON 8: THE WESTERN SOCIAL STRUCTURES..105

LESSON 9: THE CORPORATE-OWNED MASS MEDIA...119

LESSON 10: THREATS TO THE WESTERN WORLD ORDER..133

LESSON 11: WE HAVE A CHOICE..147

WORKS CITED..161

INTRODUCTION

June, 2019

These lessons represent my personal long-term process of trying to understand the true nature of U.S. foreign and domestic policy. This quest included enrolling in seven college classes—one at Metro State University taught by local peace activist, Jack Nelson-Pallmeyer, and six at the University of St. Thomas in their Justice and Peace Studies program under the direction of Rev. David Smith. I also gleaned much valuable information from library books, from Pacifica Radio's *Democracy Now!* and from various other alternative media.

I wrote the original version of these lessons for use in a discussion group in my home congregation, Christiania Lutheran Church, Lakeville, MN. Our church had hosted a visiting pastor, Benito Madembo, from the Iringa Diocese in Tanzania for a period of three weeks. For most of us, it was our first contact with a person from the Global South. We were impressed with his graciousness and beauty of spirit, but were troubled by the poverty that he and the majority of people in his homeland experienced. One of our responses was to initiate a study group seeking to understand why poverty persists in the Global South. I volunteered to lead the group, feeling it would give me an opportunity to synthesize and organize the information I had gathered from my six years of study.

I joined the Alliance for Democracy (AfD-MN) in 2000. The main emphasis of this group (no longer active) was to understand and expose the abuse of corporate power. We decided to use the lessons as part of our educational outreach. Discussion Questions, an introductory essay, and input from other AfD-MN members were added at this time.

I have long been interested in the concept of a prototype community which could model a sustainable society based on cooperation and equality that could serve as an example and incentive to all of mankind. I hope that this booklet can make a contribution to that end.

Highlighted below are two general themes that occur throughout the lessons.

1. The paradigm of the United States as a benevolent superpower is a myth.

U.S. PARADIGM

The United States is a benevolent superpower. It is our obligation, and therefore our earnest desire, to ensure peace, prosperity, freedom, and democracy, not only for U.S. citizens, but for all of humanity.

I realized during the first Gulf War (1991) that I could no longer reconcile U.S. foreign policy with the paradigm of U.S. as benevolent superpower. As U.S. citizens, we want to believe in the U.S. paradigm of benevolent superpower. We want to believe that our material wealth and our national greatness are the direct result of the form of government we instituted, the type of economic system we have developed, and the religious foundation on which our nation is built. We want to believe that we are a benevolent and caring people, that we value honesty and fairness, and that we reward initiative and hard work. Most of the people I know share these beliefs. I had accepted, without question, the paradigm of U.S. as benevolent superpower for over forty years. When that belief was shattered during the first Gulf

War, I had to ask myself, **"If not benevolence, then what is the reality of U.S. foreign policy?"** The conclusion that I eventually arrived at can be summarized in the words of Rahul Mahajan from his book *The New Crusade: America's War on Terrorism*.

U.S. REALITY

There can be no mistake about it — the United States is an empire, the most powerful in history. Empires are always about extraction of wealth from the provinces for the benefit of the center, without regard for the subject people. They may not benefit all social strata in the imperial nation — in fact, some of the lower classes have to fight and die to maintain the empire — but they always do benefit an elite. In most cases, the wealth is spread around, both among some broad strata of the imperial center, and among a native elite in the provinces, in both cases to help preserve political stability.

If the U.S. ruling class is, indeed, harboring imperial ambitions, at great cost to human rights, democratic ideals, and the natural environment, why do so many U.S. citizens continue to accept the U.S. paradigm of benevolent superpower at face value? Former AfD—MN member, David Shove, suggested the reason why the myth persists: *The myth of U.S. benevolence is the central ideological defense of the ruling class, ingrained in us by endless repetition until it seems "common sense," and thus an effective barrier to conflicting reports.* Imperialist powers seek to justify their position of dominance. The U.S. as benevolent superpower is the latest manifestation of 500 years of Western imperialism which has arrogantly proclaimed that it must shoulder "the white man's burden".

But is there more to this imperial mindset than just ruling class deception for the purpose of attaining/maintaining wealth and power? It would seem so. Former AfD-MN member, Betsy Barnum, in a Common Dreams article stated: *The United States has had, as a society, a sense of being "special" ever since people began coming to these shores looking for a place to practice their religion without oppression. The sense of America being a "promised land" has created a way of thinking about this nation that extends far beyond religious definitions. Since World War I, and especially since World War II, this sense of specialness has focused on American democracy as the highest form of democracy, something we are taught to believe it is our duty and our purpose to teach to other nations. We also view our way of life as the highest form of society and culture yet developed, characterized by individual freedom and affluence, and it is also something we believe is to be shared with the rest of the world.* The negative effects of U.S. imperialism can be easily overlooked — both by the policy-makers and the citizenry — because of this overriding internalization of specialness.

2. The biases inherent in the Western worldview of progress are devastating human solidarity and the natural environment.

Much will be said about the Western worldview of progress in the lessons, but noted here will be the negative effect its inherent biases have had, and are continuing to have, on indigenous populations and the natural environment. The state seal of Minnesota and a poem it inspired are revealing examples of these practically unconscious biases.

INTRODUCTION

Give way, give way, young warrior,
Thou and thy steed give way -
Rest not, though lingers on the hills
The red sun's parting ray
The rock bluff and prairie land
The white man claims them now,
The symbols of his course are here,
The rifle, ax and plough.

— Mary Eastman

The white European immigrant in the foreground lays claim to the land of the Native American who must therefore "give way". Why? The white man's course—progress—is regarded as superior to that of the Native American who, in fact, stands in the way of progress. The assumption is that progress will make life better. But for whom? Certainly not for the former inhabitants of the land. The gap between "developed" people and "underdeveloped" people widens and human solidarity is devastated.

The white man's symbols of progress—the rifle, ax and plough—indicate a consciousness that nonhuman life forms only have value through their use by humans. Animals are for food or sport. Nature is seen as an obstacle to be overcome and a resource to be exploited. Using the tools of modern science and technology in the quest for human benefit and financial gain, progress is accomplished by exploiting the living and nonliving resources of the planet. In the process, the natural environment is devastated.

My motivation in writing these lessons has been my belief that the human race is capable of being so much more than the current world situation would lead us to believe. Nelson Mandela, in his autobiography Long Walk to Freedom, expressed this thought: I know as well as I know anything that the oppressor must be liberated just as surely as the oppressed. The ruling elite in their desperate and misguided attempt to retain their privilege and wealth have deprived themselves of something of far greater value—the realization that individual human fulfillment can only be found in attaining a oneness with all of humanity, indeed, in attaining a oneness with all of creation as we live in harmony with each other and our natural environment.

These lessons were written by Sharon Thompson with the help and encouragement of the AfD – MN chapter and the technical help of her son-in-law, Randy Thompson.

GUIDELINES FOR STUDY CIRCLES

An optimum group size is six to eight members.

The group should decide on a convenient time and place to meet, frequency of meetings, length of time for the meeting, and who will facilitate.

It is important that each member read the assigned lesson prior to the group meeting. Write down questions or points you would like to discuss or call attention to. The Discussion Questions at the beginning of each lesson are only suggestions. Feel free to discuss questions suggested by the group.

It is recommended, but not essential, that the role of facilitator rotate among the group members. What is important is that the facilitator not be looked on as the "teacher" or "expert". His/her duties include:

- making sure that the discussion remains focused. This often requires a delicate balance — don't force the group to stick to the question at hand, but don't allow the discussion to drift too far afield.

- making sure that each person has a chance to speak. Don't allow one or two people to monopolize the discussion. If necessary, decide on a time limit per person and appoint a timekeeper. Sometimes it is necessary to ask the quieter members of the group if they have anything to add.

If more than one person wishes to speak at the same time you may want to use a "stacking" procedure. A person is designated to recognize and list in order those who wish to speak. This can be done by members simply raising their hand. Then the speakers are called on in the order listed. Points of clarification are usually allowed outside of the list order. For example, if someone does not hear or does not understand the meaning of a word used, they can ask for clarification.

Opposing viewpoints are to be expected. Respect the opinions of others.

I had always (early on) been an all-believing, rarely questioning person who accepted much of what I was told — what I was expected to believe. But the nagging doubts were always there. Inconsistencies and contradictions always appeared, and were never resolved. A plethora of books and articles appeared which fed and intensified my new direction of thought. Yet, I was yet to find anyone who had put all of the populist themes together in one coherent writing — until this year when I found a copy of Sharon Thompson's "We Have a Choice: Let's Just Do It". The sensation was much like that of a person — after months/years of traversing a desert, suddenly and miraculously — encountering a lush oasis!

- Former AfD-MN member, Max Joiner

LESSON 1:
DOMINATION – FROM LOCAL TO WORLD
DISCUSSION QUESTIONS

1. Do you agree/disagree with Riane Eisler's theory of a multilinear development of civilization?
2. In what ways would a partnership model of society be superior to a dominator model of society?
3. Did the domestication of the horse and the use of metal weapons merely speed up an inevitable process?
4. Do you agree with the contention that history is little more than a quest for more effective means of domination?
5. Do you think Jerad Diamond's "axis" theory sufficiently explains why the Global North[1] was able to dominate the Global South?
6. Do you agree/disagree with the statement that Columbus' purpose from the beginning was not mere exploration or even trade, but conquest and exploitation?
7. Is U.S. world domination a serious problem or can it lead to a more stable, peaceful world?

OTHER POINTS OF DISCUSSION

---

[1] I have chosen to use the terms Global North and Global South rather than the terms First World and Third World in designating the rich industrialized nations and the poor developing/underdeveloped nations, respectively. In direct quotes, I have retained the author's choice of terms

We live in a world of inequality — 20% of the world's population controls 80% of the world's wealth with the richest 1% controlling over 40%. How is this possible? It is possible because the richest 1% also has the ability to control what you and I think and how we look at the world around us. They are the de facto world rulers through their control of the U.S.-led, corporate-dominated global capitalist economy. They must convince those they rule over (everyone else) that this arrangement is in the best interest of all. Why is it that those who claim to rule in the name of the common good, don't?

Since the breakup of the Soviet Union in 1988, the United States has been the world's lone superpower. The similarities between the Roman Empire in the early centuries of this era and the United States today are striking. Both held/hold almost unlimited power over the other nations. Both felt/feel compelled to take on the responsibility of using this power to rule the other nations. The Roman poet Virgil reminded his fellow Romans that they had a special mission entrusted to them by the gods:

> *To rule the people under law, to establish*
> *The way of peace, to battle down the haughty,*
> *To spare the meek, Our fine arts, these, forever.*

Compare these words to those of President Lyndon Johnson: *Of course, security and welfare shape our policies. But much of the energy of our efforts has come from moral purpose. It is right that the strong should help the weak defend their freedom. It is right that nations should be free from the coercion of others.* (August 1964)

As is all too often the case, the beautiful words used to describe U.S. national purpose do not match the governmental policies that are then undertaken. President Johnson's words were delivered as his administration prepared to use U.S. military force to intervene in the affairs of Vietnam — not for the benefit of the largely peasant population — but at great cost to them and their environment. The beneficiaries of the Vietnam War were intended to be large U.S. corporations. The words of Undersecretary of State U. Alexis Johnson, as he spoke to the Economic Club of Detroit (1963), give us a much clearer picture: *What is the attraction that Southeast Asia has exerted for centuries on the great powers flanking it on all sides? Why is it desirable, and why is it important? The countries of Southeast Asia produce rich exportable surpluses such as rice, rubber, teak, corn, tin, spices, oil, and many others.* In other words: these countries could provide an abundance of cheap resources for large U.S. corporations if their governments were to become U.S.-friendly.

Can anyone or any group with the power to do so, rule others in a just and beneficial way? If the ruling elite of today are a representative example, then the answer is "No". Can we find a way that the ordinary people of the world can rule themselves in the best interest of all? We stand at a crossroads in human history. The course we are on can only lead to further degradation of the environment, greater social dysfunction, increased violence, and the extinction of our species. The choice seems simple: Let's just do it!

LESSON 1: DOMINATION – FROM LOCAL TO WORLD 15

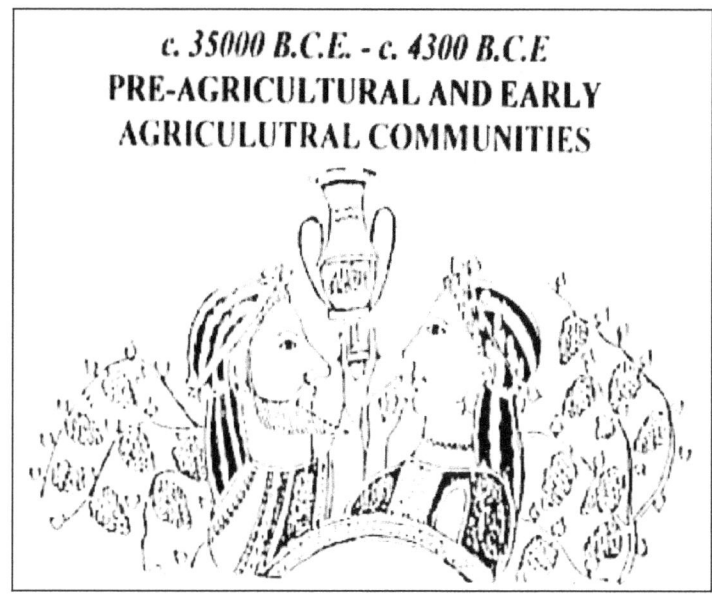

Note: I have chosen this ancient piece of artwork to represent the partnership model of society. It depicts the god Dionysus and the goddess Semele surrounded by the fruit of nature. They form a partnership, with neither figure dominant over the other. The chalice represents the life-generating and nurturing powers of the earth. It should be contrasted with the later artwork (below) which glorifies violence and domination.

PARTNERSHIP MODEL OF SOCIETY

DOMINATOR MODEL OF SOCIETY

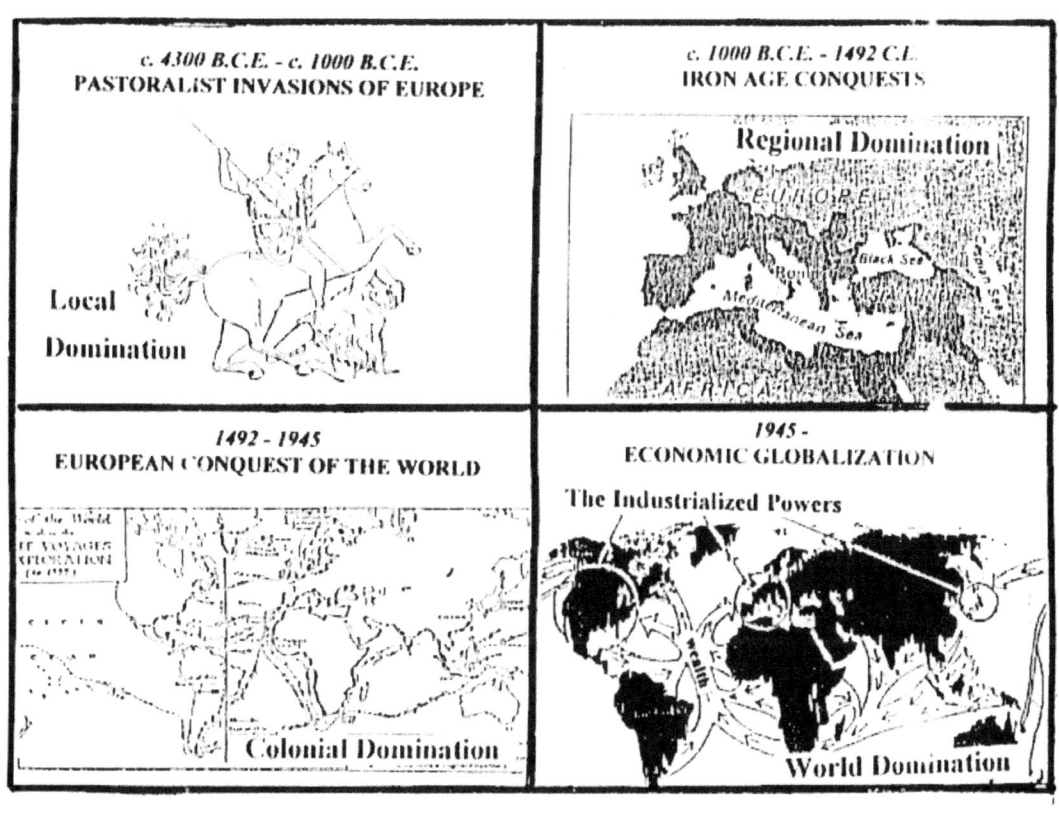

LESSON 1: DOMINATION – FROM LOCAL TO WORLD

CALENDAR PAGE c.35000 B.C.E. - c.4300 B.C.E.: PRE-AGRICULTURAL AND EARLY AGRICULTURAL COMMUNITIES (PARTNERSHIP MODEL OF SOCIETY):

While *a hierarchical and patriarchal* system based on domination and violence has been the cultural norm for the last 5,000 years, it has not always been this way. There is compelling evidence that human civilization developed in a variety of forms, including one that was characterized by cooperation and shared decision-making between men and women and among related and non-related clans and tribes. This *"partnership" model of society* survived well into the Bronze Age such as in the Minoan civilization of Crete (c.3000 B.C.E. - 1100 B.C.E.). If this is true, what changed and why?

JAGGED LINE:

Human progress is disrupted as the partnership model of society is replaced with a dominator model of society.

CALENDAR PAGE c.4300 B.C.E. - c.1000 B.C.E.: PASTORALIST INVASIONS OF EUROPE (LOCAL DOMINATION):

A *"dominator" model of society* — hierarchical, patriarchal, and war-like — developed in areas where pastoral peoples were subjected to a harsh struggle for survival. Aided by the domestication of the horse (c. 5000 B.C.E.) and the use of metal weapons, pastoralist nomads conquered the partnership communities and imposed their dominator model of society on them.

CALENDAR PAGE c.1000 B.C.E. - 1492 C.E.: IRON AGE CONQUESTS (REGIONAL DOMINATION):

Empire building was introduced at the dawn of the *Iron Age* (c.1000 B.C.E.) with its innovations in military techniques and leadership. Iron weapons, especially the horse-drawn chariot, allowed for a more powerful and mobile military. Dynastic monarchs, claiming to rule by divine right, were able to extend their domination beyond their local area to a larger regional area.

CALENDAR PAGE 1492 – 1945: THE EUROPEAN CONQUEST OF THE WORLD (COLONIAL DOMINATION):

The Western European nations began the process whereby technologically superior nations dominated "undeveloped" areas of the world. They accomplished this by establishing colonial empires.

CALENDAR PAGE 1945 - : U.S.- LED ECONOMIC GLOBALIZATION (WORLD DOMINATION):

The Colonial Domination era came to an end when competition among the colonial masters for natural resources and markets for industrial output resulted in the devastation of World Wars I and II. The use of the atomic bomb, by the U.S. near the end of World War II, made war among the industrialized nations no longer feasible. At this time, the U.S., in a po-

LESSON 1: DOMINATION – FROM LOCAL TO WORLD

sition of unprecedented economic, military, and political power, began a process of world domination through *economic globalization*. This would require that the wealth of the *Global South* (the former colonies) would continue to flow to the *Global North* (the industrialized nations) which the U.S. version of a global economy would ensure.

CALENDAR PAGE c.35,000 B.C.E – c.4300 B.C.E.: PRE-AGRICULTURAL AND EARLY AGRICULTURAL COMMUNITIES (PARTNERSHIP MODEL OF SOCIETY):

While a *hierarchical and patriarchal* system based on domination and violence has been the cultural norm for the last 5,000 years, it has not always been this way. There is compelling evidence that human civilization developed in a variety of forms, including one that was characterized by cooperation and shared decision-making between men and women and among related and non-related clans and tribes. This *"partnership" model of society* survived well into the *Bronze Age* such as in the Minoan civilization of Crete (c.3000 B.C.E. - c.1100 B.C.E.). [Note: The terminology and concept of the contrasting models of society, "partnership" and "dominator," are taken from Riane Eisler's book *The Chalice and the Blade*.]

Riane Eisler in her books, *The Chalice & the Blade and Sacred Pleasure*, is a proponent of this multilinear concept of civilization development. She describes early agricultural civilization as a virtual "Garden of Eden" existence with men and women living in harmony with each other and nature. She explains: *The prehistoric societies that developed in the more fertile areas of our globe (where nature could be seen as a life-giving and sustaining mother and agriculture could gradually replace gathering-hunting) probably originally oriented primarily to the partnership model. In these areas, the veneration of the feminine creative principle eventually flourished, and myths and rites of alignment with the life-generating creative powers of nature such as the* **hieros gamos**, *or sacred sexual union, first developed.* If this thesis is correct, what changed and why?

JAGGED LINE:

Human progress is disrupted as the partnership model of society is replaced with a dominator model of society.

CALENDAR PAGE c 4300 B.C.E. - c.1000 B.C.E.: PASTORALIST INVASIONS OF EUROPE (LOCAL DOMINATION):

"dominator" model of society — hierarchical, patriarchal, and war-like — developed in areas where pastoral peoples were subjected to a harsh struggle for survival. Aided by the domestication of the horse (c. 5000 B.C.E.) and the use of metal weapons, pastoralist nomads conquered the partnership communities and imposed their dominator model of society on them. Eisler explains: *In the less hospitable, more marginal areas of our globe, the powers that govern the universe would have been seen as far more harsh. Indeed, because of the hardship and suffering one had to chronically endure, they would often have been seen as punitive. Thus, rituals would have tended to be less rites to attempt alignment with the beneficial forces of nature than attempts to somehow placate and otherwise control the unreliable, seemingly angry, destructive forces of nature. And here, especially during times of acute scarcity, hierarchies based on fear and force would have been far more likely to evolve.* Eisler defines this "dominator" model of social organization as: *a social system in which male dominance, male violence, and a generally hierarchic and authoritarian social structure was the norm.*

For millennia, these two contrasting types of social organization coexisted, with the partnership model being the more prevalent. Two things occurred that would change this status quo: 1) the domestication of large mammals, first the sheep and goat, by pastoral nomads served to deplete the already not-so-fertile areas of the globe; 2) climatic changes intensified this process and led to armed conflict between nomadic tribes for the precious water and vegetation that remained. With the domestication of the horse (c. 5000 B.C.E.), nomadic pastoral tribes could, and did, invade and conquer the basically defenseless agricultural partnership communities.

Eisler contrasts the two types of social systems: *How fundamentally different these two social systems were, and how cataclysmic were the norm-changes forced by these "peripheral isolates" – now become "peripheral invaders" – is summarized in the following passage from* [archeologist Marija] *Gimbutas's work* [First Wave of Eurasian Steppe Pastoralists]: *"The Old European* [agricultural communities] *and Kurgan* [Eurasian steppe pastoralists] *cultures were the antithesis of one another. The Old European were sedentary horticulturists prone to live in large well-planned townships. The absence of fortifications and weapons attests the peaceful coexistence of this egalitarian civilization that was probably matrilineal* [inheriting or determining descent through the female line] *and matrilocal* [of or pertaining to residence with the wife's family or tribe]. *The Kurgan system was composed of patrilineal, socially stratified, herding units which lived in small villages or seasonal settlements while grazing their animals over vast areas. One economy based on farming, the other on stock breeding and grazing, produced two contrasting ideologies. The Old European belief system focused on the agricultural cycle of birth, death, and regeneration, embodied in the female principle, a Mother Creatrix. The Kurgan ideology, as known from comparative Indo-European mythology, exalted virile, heroic warrior gods of the shining and thunderous sky. Weapons are nonexistent in Old European imagery; whereas the dagger and battle-axe are dominant symbols of the Kurgans, who like all historically known Indo-Europeans, glorified the lethal power of the sharp blade.*

Eisler describes the first wave of nomadic pastoral (Kurgan) invasions (c. 4300 B.C.E. - 4200 B.C.E.): *Spreading westward and southward* [from the steppe region north of the Black Sea and Caspian Sea in present day Ukraine and Russia], *the archeological landscape of Old Europe is now traumatically altered. "Millennial traditions were truncated," writes Gimbutas, "towns and villages disintegrated, magnificent painted pottery vanished; as did shrines, frescoes, sculptures, symbols, and script." At the same time there now comes into play a new living war machine, the armed man on a horse - which in its time must have had the impact a tank or an airplane has among primitives in ours. And in the wake of the Kurgan devastation, we find their typical warrior-chieftain graves, with their human sacrifices of women and children, their animal sacrifices, and their caches of weapons surrounding the dead chiefs.*

Eisler cites another expert: *European prehistorian V. Gordon Childe describes the same general pattern. Childe characterizes the culture of early Europeans as "peaceful" and "democratic", with no hint of "chiefs concentrating the communities' wealth." But then he notes how all this gradually changed, as warfare, and particularly the use of metal weapons, is introduced. Like Gimbutas, Childe observes that as weapons increasingly appear in the excavations, so do chief's tombs and houses that clearly evidence social stratification, with strongman rule becoming the norm. "Settlements were often planted on hill tops," writes Childe. Both there and in the valleys, they are now "frequently fortified". Moreover, he too emphasizes that, as "competition for land assumed a bellicose character, and weapons such as battle-axes became specialized for warfare," not only the social, but also the ideological organization of European society underwent a fundamental alteration.*

LESSON 1: DOMINATION — FROM LOCAL TO WORLD

Eisler describes the effects on the Old European settlements as *"catastrophic"*. *There is wholesale destruction of houses, shrines, of finely crafted artifacts, and works of art. Masses of people are massacred, enslaved, or put to flight. Now what Gimbutas calls "hybrid cultures" begin to appear. These cultures were based on the subjugation of remaining Old European groups and their rapid assimilation into the Kurgan pastoral and patrilinear stratified societies. But these new hybrid cultures are far less technologically and culturally advanced than the cultures they replace. And fortifications now begin to appear everywhere, as gradually the acropolis or hill fort replaces the old unwalled settlement.*

And so, as prehistoric excavations evidence, the archaeological landscape of Old Europe is transformed. Not only do we find increasing signs of physical destruction and cultural regression in the wake of each wave of invasions; the direction of cultural history is also profoundly altered. Slowly, as the Old Europeans, for the most part unsuccessfully, try to protect themselves from their barbaric invaders, new definitions of what is normal for both society and ideology begin to emerge. **Everywhere now we see the shift in social priorities that is like an arrow shot through time to pierce our age with its nuclear tip; the shift toward more effective technologies of destruction.** *(Emphasis added.) This is accomplished by a fundamental ideological shift. The power to dominate and destroy through the sharp blade gradually supplants the view of power as the capacity to support and nurture life. For not only was the evolution of the earlier partnership civilizations truncated by armed conquests; those societies that were not simply wiped out were now also radically changed. Now everywhere the men with the greatest power to destroy — the physically strongest, most insensitive, most brutal — rise to the top, as everywhere the social structure becomes more hierarchic and authoritarian. Women - who as a group are physically smaller and weaker than men, and who are most closely identified with the old view of power symbolized by the life-giving and sustaining chalice — are now gradually reduced to the status they are to hold hereafter: male-controlled technologies of production and reproduction.*

Thus, at a specific time in our prehistory — the fifth millennium B.C.E. — domination became the rule of the day. Men dominated women, the powerful few dominated the masses, and the human species dominated all other animals and the natural environment. In the settled, agricultural areas, this dominator model of society replaced tens of thousands of years of peaceful and cooperative development and civilization. And so it has remained up to the present day. What has changed in the last 5,000 years is the geographic range of the dominators as those in power have developed ever greater means to subdue ever greater numbers of people. The early dominator societies were confined to their local areas. However, this was to change with the discovery and use of iron.

CALENDAR PAGE c.1000 B.C.E. - 1492 C.E.: IRON AGE CONQUESTS (REGIONAL DOMINATION):

Empire building was introduced at the dawn of the ***Iron Age*** (c.1000 B.C.E.) with its innovations in military techniques and leadership. Iron weapons, especially the horse-drawn chariot, allowed for a more powerful and mobile military. Dynastic monarchs, claiming to rule by divine right, were able to extend their domination beyond their local area to a larger regional area. They replaced the more stationary priest-kings and strong-men of the local settlements. The Assyrian, Babylonian, Persian, Greek, and Roman Empires enter human history and are used as models for later empire builders. But domination by regional empires was to give way to domination through colonial empires. Technology — this time advances in navigation, in weapons (especially guns) and in other areas — once again played a major role. The age of

Western European colonialism—domination over far-away lands and people—was about to begin.

CALENDAR PAGE 1492-1945: THE EUROPEAN CONQUEST OF THE WORLD (COLONIAL DOMINATION):

The Western European nations began the process whereby technologically superior nations dominate and exploit the people and resources of "undeveloped" areas of the world. They accomplished this by establishing colonial empires. The industrialized nations of Western Europe were able to protect their own industries while preventing industrialization in their colonies, or in some cases such as India, destroying the existing industries. They managed to retain a monopoly on technology and to set the terms of trade to their advantage.

Western European colonial domination began in the fifteenth century when **Christopher Columbus**, sailing on behalf of Spain, inadvertently "discovered" the Western Hemisphere. Although every school child has been taught that Columbus was a great explorer and that he was seeking an alternate trade route to the East, James W. Loewen in his book *Lies My Teacher Told Me* disagrees: *His* [Columbus'] *purpose from the beginning was not mere exploration or even trade, but conquest and exploitation, for which he used religion as a rationale.* He claimed the newly discovered lands for the Christian nation of Spain. Portugal quickly imitated Spain in its colonization and exploitation of the "New World".

To avoid war between the two Catholic countries of Portugal and Spain over control of the Western Hemisphere and elsewhere, **Pope Alexander VI** divided the world between them by drawing the *Line of Demarcation* in 1494. This initiated the age of European colonization with England, France and the Netherlands (non-Catholic countries which did not recognize the authority of the pope) soon following Spain and Portugal's lead. Later, Germany, Belgium, and Italy also became colonial masters.

Eurocentrism and a belief in the divine sanction of their "civilizing" mission to the indigenous peoples led to the dehumanization of conquered peoples and allowed for their exploitation. European merchants, capitalists, and industrialists, with the backing of their governments and with the sanction of the church took the lead in establishing the colonial empires. They established the West African slave trade when the enslaving of Native Americans proved unsuccessful. Later, when the tide of public opinion turned against the slave trade, they would justify establishing colonies in Africa with the argument that they were doing so to rid the continent of the slave trade.

While we can speak of the European conquest of the world as occurring in the last 500 years, the advantages that the early European explorers and conquerors held over the peoples they vanquished has a much longer history. Jared Diamond in his book, *Guns, Germs, and Steel* asks the question: *Why did Europeans reach and conquer the lands of Native Americans instead of vice versa?* His one sentence answer is: *Again and again, people with access to the prerequisites for food production, and with a location favoring diffusion of technology from elsewhere, replaced peoples lacking these advantages.* There is not a hint in his explanation that the conquerors possessed superior intelligence or were morally superior in any way to the peoples they vanquished. Rather, Diamond explains that their advantage resulted solely from an accident of geography.

What are the "prerequisites for food production" and what is "a location favoring diffusion of technology from elsewhere" and why are they such an advantage? Diamond asserts that the causative factor is the axis, or predominant direction, (east and west or north and south) in which an area lies. He breaks this down by continents, treating Europe and Asia, along with northern Africa (Eurasia) as one unit, the Americas as another, and Africa as the third. The map illustrates these axes:

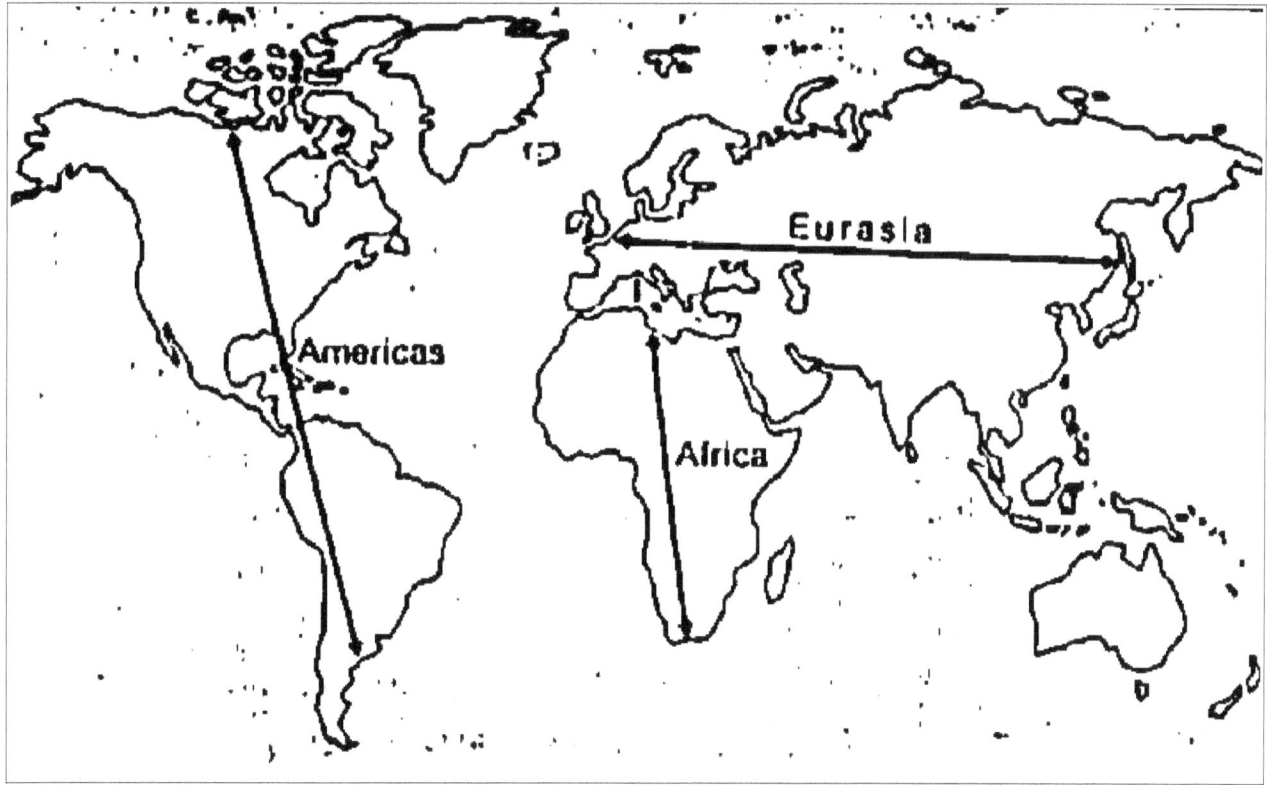

The axis of Eurasia is east and west while that of the Americas and Africa are north and south. Although food production started independently in all these areas, Eurasia produced the greatest variety and most nutritious domesticated plants and, because of its east-west axis, food production easily spread from its origins in China and southwest Asia across the vast Eurasian landmass. This was due primarily to similar climatic conditions (length of day, temperature, rainfall, etc.) and the absence of major geographical barriers. In contrast, the three areas of independent food production in the Americas—the Eastern United States, Central America, and the Andean area of South America—never came into contact with each other due to climatic differences and natural geographic barriers (the Mexican desert and the tropical rain forest). Likewise, southern Africa was isolated from northern Africa by the tropical rain forest and the Sahara Desert. Thus, the first factor in acquiring the prerequisites of food production, a variety of plants suitable for domestication, were more readily available to the peoples of the Eurasian landmass than to either the peoples of the Americas or southern Africa.

An integral part of food production, as well as bestowing other benefits, is the domestication of large mammals. Eurasia produced all five of the major species of domesticated large mammals—sheep, goats, cattle, pigs, and horses. The other nine species of domesticated large mammals were each restricted to a small area and were of limited use. The advantages that domesticated large mammals gave the Eurasians were: 1) they provided the chief source of animal protein (meat and milk); 2) they enhanced crop production by drawing plows and providing manure; 3) they provided wool and hides; 4) they were the main mode of land transport of people and goods; 5) they were vehicles of warfare; and 6) they were sources of "industrial" power. Thus, the peoples of Eurasia were able to further their advantage in acquiring the prerequisites of food production by the domestication and diffusion of large mammals across the vast landmass they occupied, while, with the lone exception of the llama in Peru, in the Americas and southern Africa there were no large mammals suitable for domestication.

As food production increased, food surpluses and storage led to larger, denser, sedentary, societies. This had two major effects: 1) **political organization** became more complex allowing for increasing specialization including people who mastered the skill of **writing**; 2) as more people were released from food production, **technology** became more prevalent. Whereas in the Americas the inventors of the wheel (for use on toys only) never came into contact with the people who domesticated the llama (because of the obstacles inherent in their north-south axis), in Eurasia there was a free flow of ideas and technology back and forth among many different groups. Diamond explains how medieval Islam, being centrally located, benefited by this exchange of information and technology from all directions — India to the south ("Arabic" numerals, an indispensable tool of modern science and technology), China to the east (paper and gunpowder) and Greek literature from the west. *It [Islam] achieved far higher literacy rates than contemporary Europe; it assimilated the legacy of classical Greek civilization to such a degree that many classical Greek books are now known to us only through Arabic copies; it invented or elaborated windmills, tidal mills, trigonometry, and lateen sails; it made major advances in metallurgy, mechanical and chemical engineering, and irrigation methods; and it adopted paper and gunpowder from China and transmitted them to Europe. In the Middle Ages the flow of technology was overwhelmingly from Islam to Europe, rather than from Europe to Islam as it is today. Only after around 1500 C.E. did the net direction of flow begin to reverse.* Thus, the peoples of Eurasia had a great advantage over the peoples of the Americas and southern Africa because they resided in a "location favoring diffusion of technology from elsewhere".

The combination of domesticated plants and animals and a sedentary population had a down side as Diamond explains: *diverse **epidemic diseases** of humans evolved in areas with many wild plant and animal species suitable for domestication, partly because the resulting crops and livestock helped feed dense societies in which epidemics could maintain themselves, and partly because the diseases evolved from germs of the domestic animals themselves.* But this gave the Europeans a decided advantage when they came in contact with the Native Americans. Having no genetic or acquired resistance to European diseases, some have estimated that as much as 95% of the Native American population succumbed to smallpox, measles, influenza, typhus, diphtheria, mumps, pertussis, tuberculosis, and other epidemic diseases. Add to this the advantages of the Europeans being backed by a centralized government, the use of writing as a means to communicate, the means to cross the Atlantic Ocean, the superiority of European soldiers on horseback with steel swords, armor, and guns over Native American foot soldiers with primitive weapons and lacking armor and it becomes apparent why the Europeans conquered the peoples of America rather than vice versa.

Why didn't other Eurasian countries "jump on the bandwagon" of colonization? In the case of Japan, it had chosen a policy of isolation during that period, which, being an island was a viable option. Also, the powerful Samurai class rejected the use of guns, preferring the use of swords for their traditional and aesthetic value. China, an ancient and technologically advanced civilization, for various reasons, had chosen to abandon its maritime ventures, while Russia had the disadvantage of not having a warm water port.

LESSON 1: DOMINATION – FROM LOCAL TO WORLD

Why did European epidemic diseases affect Native Americans and New World epidemic diseases not affect Europeans? The reason was simple—there were no New World (or Australian) epidemic diseases. With the exception of the llama in Peru, Native Americans had no contact with domesticated animals from which most of the diseases originated and they lived in less densely populated areas which would not have supported epidemic diseases. But epidemic diseases did not act solely to the Europeans' advantage. Diamond continues: *While the New World and Australia did not have native epidemic diseases awaiting Europeans, tropical Asia, Africa, Indonesia, and New Guinea certainly did. Malaria throughout the tropical Old World, cholera in tropical Southeast Asia, and yellow fever in tropical Africa were (and still are) the most notorious of the tropical killers. They posed the most serious obstacle to European colonization of the tropics, and they explain why the European partitioning of New Guinea and most of Africa was not accomplished until nearly 400 years after European partitioning of the New World began. Furthermore, once malaria and yellow fever did become transmitted to the Americans by European ship traffic, they emerged as the major impediment to colonialization of the New World tropics as well. A familiar example is the role of those two diseases in aborting the French effort, and nearly aborting the ultimately successful American effort, to construct the Panama Canal.*

Europeans had other motives for establishing colonies besides the exploitation of resources and labor and establishing markets for their industrial production. There was a desire to spread what was felt to be a superior culture and to proselytize for religion. But one of the objectives of these activities was to undermine the existing culture and social structures of the colonies which complemented the efforts of the colonizers.

CALENDAR PAGE 1945 – U.S.-LED ECONOMIC GLOBALIZATION (WORLD DOMINATION):

The Colonial Domination era came to an end when competition among the colonial masters for natural resources and markets for industrial output resulted in the devastation of World Wars I and II. The use of the atomic bomb, by the United States near the end of World War II, made war among the industrialized nations no longer feasible. At this time, the United States, in a position of unprecedented economic, military, and political power, began a process of world domination through the means of ***economic globalization.***

It is important to understand that the United States is unlike any other nation state. In his book *Overthrow* Stephen Kinzer states: *There is no stronger or more persistent strain in the American character than the belief that the United States is a nation uniquely endowed with virtue. Americans consider themselves to be, in Herman Melville's words, "a peculiar, chosen people, the Israel of our times." In a nation too new to define itself by real or imagined historical triumphs, and too diverse to be bound together by a shared religion or ethnicity, this belief became the essence of national identity, the conviction that bound Americans to each other and defined their approach to the world.*

Kinzer continues: *This view is driven by a profound conviction that the American form of government, based on capitalism and individual political choice, is, as President Bush asserted, "right and true for every person in every society"....A clear truth lies behind this belief in the transformative value of American influence. For more than a century, Americans have believed they deserve access to markets and resources in other countries. When they are denied that access, they take what they want by force, deposing governments that stand in their way. Great powers have done this since time immemorial.* **What distinguishes Americans from citizens of past empires is their eagerness to persuade themselves that they are acting out of humanitarian motives.**

So how did this unique belief system affect the U.S. approach to setting up a global economy? The U.S. version of a global economy, supported by their Western allies, would require that the wealth of the *Global South* (the former colonies) would continue to flow to the *Global North* (the industrialized nations). That this would most likely result in an anti-American/anti-Western reaction, rather than a pro-American/pro-Western reaction, seemingly escaped the planners of economic globalization.

Economic globalization represents the ultimate stage of a dominator society—world domination. The next lesson looks at that system and its ramifications.

LESSON 2:
ECONOMIC GLOBALIZATION
DISCUSSION QUESTIONS

1. What is your sense of who controls world events or does no one?

2. Why do you think the Global North elite choose to remain "invisible"?

3. Do you think that economic globalization could be accomplished in a fair and equitable manner? Why or why not?

4. Are you aware of the influence that think tanks have on the formation of public policy? Who funds them and why?

5. Why can't the nations of the Global South follow the example of the nations of the Global North in their economic development?

6. What is your understanding of the purpose of the Council on Foreign Relations? The Bilderberg? The trilateral Commission? Or have you never heard of them?

7. What is an alternative to economic globalization as currently practiced? Or is there none?

OTHER POINTS OF DISCUSSION

World War II marked the end of one era and the beginning of another as the mantle of world economic leadership passed from Great Britain to the United States. There were some U.S. policy-planners who saw this as an opportunity to end the twin specters of war and poverty once and for all. The rapid advances in technology would make it possible for the earth's abundance to meet the needs of all people everywhere, ushering in an era of "peace through prosperity". This view was expressed in a 1944 speech by Henry Morgenthau, U.S. Secretary of the Treasury, at the UN Monetary and Financial Conference which was convened to plan for the post-war global economy. He foresaw: *the creation of a dynamic world economy in which the peoples of every nation will be able to realize their potentialities in peace and enjoy increasingly the fruits of material progress on an earth infinitely blessed with natural riches.*

The opposing view—that the United States should take full advantage of its economic dominance to reshape the world to its own benefit (or, more accurately, the benefit of its corporations)—won the day. George Kennan, head of the State Department's planning staff, in a 1948 confidential planning paper (Policy Planning Study 23), exemplified this view: *...We have about 50% of the world's wealth, but only 6.3% of its population... In this situation, we cannot fail to be the object of envy and resentment. Our real task in the coming period is to devise a pattern of relationships which will permit us to maintain this position of disparity without positive detriment to our national security. To do so we have to dispense with all sentimentality and day-dreaming; and our attention will have to be concentrated everywhere on our immediate national objectives. We need not deceive ourselves that we can afford today the luxury of altruism and world-benefaction....We should cease to talk about vague and...unreal objectives such as human rights, the raising of the living standards and democratization. The day is not far off when we are going to have to deal in straight power concepts. The less we are hampered by idealistic slogans, the better.* This policy has guided all U.S. post-war administrations, albeit, with the rhetoric of world benefaction.

Following the war, major U.S. corporations dictated U.S. economic policy worldwide, and these policies were backed by the U.S. military. They demanded access to the raw materials, markets, and labor in the formerly colonized areas of the world. The existence of the Soviet Union posed the major deterrent to U.S. corporate global ambitions, but it also brought Europe and Japan (the other leading capitalist powers) into military alliances with the U.S. which reinforced U.S. hegemony over these economic competitors. The Cold War provided a cover" for U.S. imperialistic designs, as well—it could all be done in the name of "containing Communism". The breakup of the Soviet bloc in 1989 marked the beginning of a "new world order". However, this time, "peace through prosperity" was not even on the agenda. The policy debate was simply: How do we best exploit the fact that the U.S. is now the world's only superpower? Do we act unilaterally or multilaterally? Do we engage in nation-building or not? And so on and so forth. The U.S. policy objective of economic globalization, which has been in place for over fifty years, is no longer constrained by Cold War considerations.

LESSON 2: ECONOMIC GLOBALIZATION

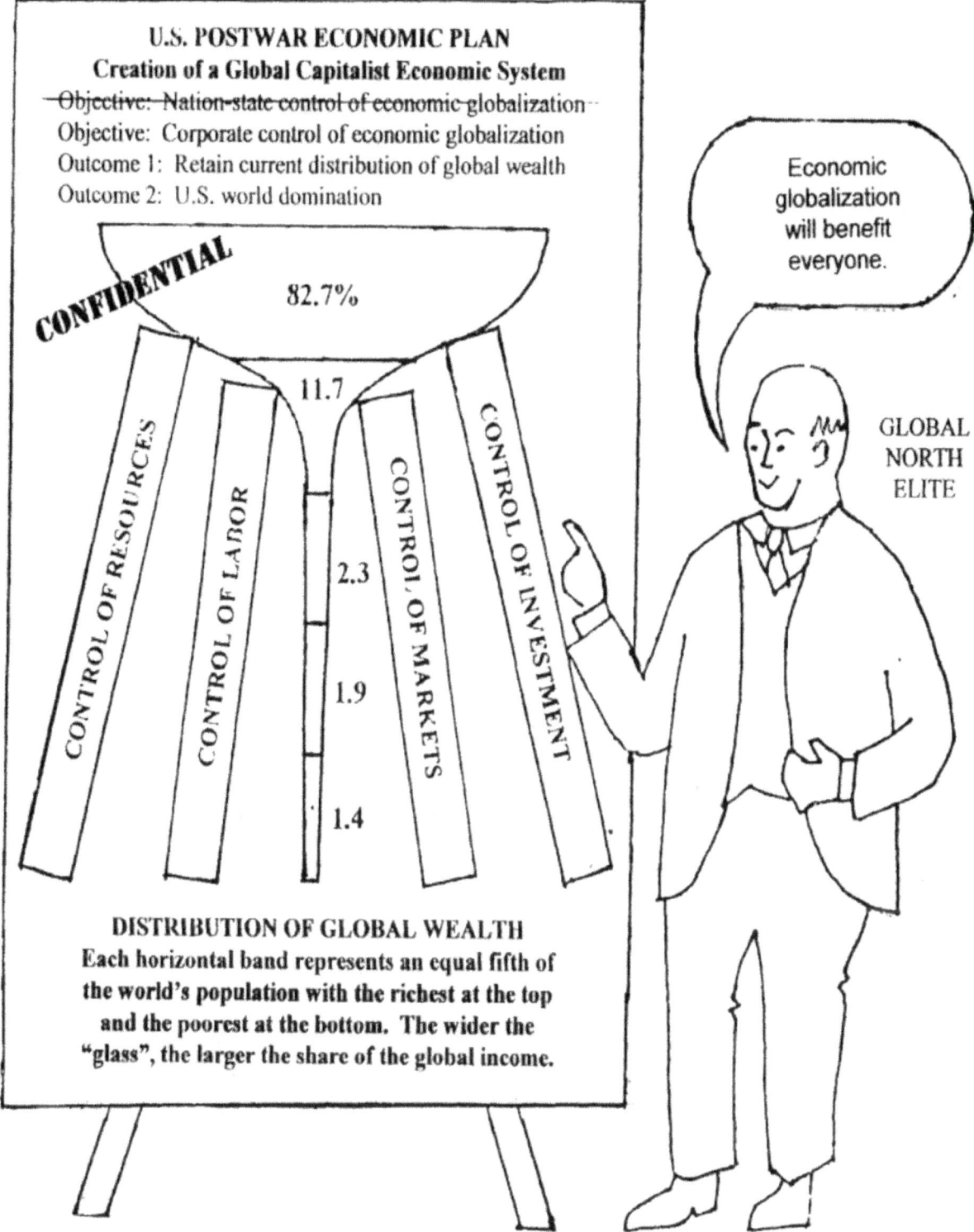

CHART:

U.S. post-WW II economic plan. Realizing that wealthy, industrialized nation-states competing for resources and markets was no longer a viable option in attaining world stability, U.S. post-war planners and other Western elites called for the creation of a system of economic globalization which would integrate the world's economies into a single capitalist system. This would allow for cooperation among the industrialized nations and yet would retain control of world resources and markets for the benefit of the Global North.

CROSSED-OUT OBJECTIVE:

As indicated by the change in the "Objective" (from nation-state control to corporate control) in time, control of this system shifted from the nation-states to large, primarily U.S., transnational corporations and other monied interests. The desired "Outcomes" would remain the same.

"CHAMPAGNE GLASS" DEPICTION OF GLOBAL WEALTH:

This plan for economic globalization would retain the inequitable distribution of wealth created by the European conquest of the world.

FOUR PILLARS SUPPORT THE UNSTABLE STRUCTURE OF WEALTH DISTRIBUTION:

People do not willingly allow their wealth to be appropriated by others. It is accomplished through the economic, military, and technological advantage that the nations of the Global North hold over the nations of the Global South. This advantage allows Global North control of the resources, labor, markets, and investment opportunities of the Global South. Economic globalization was to be accomplished by imposing a global capitalist system. Neoliberal policy which adheres to Free Market principles became the method of choice under U.S. President Ronald Reagan and U.K. Prime Minister Margaret Thatcher.

FIGURE:

The Global North elite. This small group of people consists of those individuals who make up the ruling classes of the Global North nations. They are those powerful forces in industry, banking and commerce who de facto rule the world. These nations are the United States (in the position of leadership), Western Europe, and Japan. They operate through a variety of forums to pursue their common interests. Considering the vast amount of power they wield, they remain virtually invisible to the great majority of people. This is intentional since elite interests are diametrically opposed to those of ordinary people, both in the Global South and the Global North.

MESSAGE IN SPEECH BALLOON AND "CONFIDENTIAL" STAMP:

While loudly proclaiming the benefits of economic globalization, the methods used to accomplish it (the pillars supporting the glass) are not for public consumption.

LESSON 2: ECONOMIC GLOBALIZATION

CHART:

U.S. - led post-WW II economic plan. Realizing that wealthy, industrialized nation-states competing for resources and markets was no longer a viable option for attaining world stability, U.S. postwar planners and other Western elites called for the creation of a system of *economic globalization* which would integrate the world's economies into a single *capitalist* system. This would allow for cooperation among the industrialized nations and yet would retain control of world resources and markets for the benefit of the Global North.

CROSSED-OUT OBJECTIVE:

As indicated by the change in the "Objective" (from nation-state control to corporate control) in time, control of this system shifted from the nation-states to large, primarily U.S., transnational corporations and other monied interests. The desired "Outcomes" would remain the same.

"CHAMPAGNE GLASS" DEPICTION OF THE DISTRIBUTION OF GLOBAL WEALTH:

[The source for the "champagne glass" depiction of global wealth is *UNDP Human Development Report, 1992*.] This plan for economic globalization would retain the inequitable distribution of wealth created by the European conquest of the world.

FOUR PILLARS SUPPORT THE UNSTABLE STRUCTURE OF WEALTH DISTRIBUTION:

People do not willingly allow their wealth to be appropriated by others. It is accomplished through the economic, military, and technological advantage that the nations of the Global North hold over the nations of the Global South. This advantage allows the Global North control of the resources, labor, markets, and investment opportunities of the Global South. Economic globalization was to be accomplished by imposing a global capitalist system. Neoliberal policy which adheres to Free Market principles became the method of choice under U.S. President Ronald Reagan and U.K. Prime Minister Margaret Thatcher.

Note: Today, **liberalism** is generally thought of as state intervention to ensure widespread economic security. However, Soya Jung in an article entitled "Neoliberals and Neocons: What's the Difference, And Why Should I Care? (Race Files 11/27/12) states: *Neoliberalism was in fact an [elite] class backlash against what we think of as liberal policies like the welfare and public works programs that were created in response to the Great Depression. President Franklin D. Roosevelt enacted "New Deal" programs in the 1930's to provide relief to the poor, to stimulate the economy, and to reform the financial sector to avoid another depression.* Thus, neoliberalism is not a "new" Liberalism, but rather its opposite – an attack on liberal policies. While Neoliberalism is primarily concerned with economic policy, Neoconservatism, is a U.S. political philosophy which advocates an active foreign policy, including use of military intervention. Jung continues: *This includes the idea of preemptive attack – that the United States has the right to attack governments that pose potential threats to U.S. security, even if those threats aren't immediate.* Often, neoliberal and neoconservative agendas overlap.

What is the origin of "free market" ideology that modern-day neoliberalism rests on? In the book, *Understanding Power: The Indispensable Chomsky* (edited by Peter R. Mitchell and John Schoeffel), Noam Chomsky explains that "free market" ideology is nothing new. Its origins can be traced back to the needs of the emerging capitalist class in England at the dawn of the industrial revolution: *You see, during the early stages of the industrial revolution, as England was coming out of a feudal-type society and into what's basically a state-capitalist system, the rising bourgeoisie there had a problem. In a traditional society like the feudal system, people had a certain place, and they had certain rights - in fact, they had what was called at the time a "right to live". I mean, under feudalism it may have been a lousy right, but nevertheless people were assumed to have some natural entitlement for survival. But with the rise of what we call capitalism, that right had to be destroyed: people had to have it knocked out of their heads that they had any automatic "right to live" beyond what they could win for themselves on the labor market. And that was the main point of* **classical economics**.

Chomsky continues: *Classical economists, such as [Thomas] Malthus [1766-1834] and David Ricardo [1772-1823] argued that you only harm the poor by making them believe that they have rights other than what they can win on the market, like a basic right to live, because that kind of right interferes with the market, and with efficiency, and with growth and so on – so ultimately people will just be worse off if you try to recognize them.* Chomsky then explains that as living conditions worsened for the masses, having been driven off the land by the **Enclosure Laws** and deprived of basic necessities by the repeal of the **Poor Laws** (laws that provided a minimum level of subsistence), they turned to rioting and organizing themselves in protest, while many others emigrated to the United States and Australia at this time. The capitalist elite, recognizing the threat to their right to rule, turned to a more **social-democratic** economic ideology to appease the masses. However, in recent years the old **laissez faire** ideology of the early English capitalist class ("hands off" the economy if it benefits ordinary people, but economic intervention to benefit big business) has been revived under the guise of **neoliberal** economic globalization.

So what exactly is neoliberal economic globalization? And what do its proponents hope to accomplish? In an article "Neoliberals and economic globalization (Share the World's Resources 11/23/06) Rajesh Makwana writes: *The goal of neoliberal economic globalization is the removal of all barriers to commerce, and the privatization of all available resources and services. Neoliberal policies advocate market forces and commercial activity as the most efficient methods for producing and supplying goods and services. At the same time they shun the role of the state and discourage government intervention into economic, financial and even social affairs. The process of economic globalization is driven by this ideology: removing borders and barriers between nations so that market forces can drive the global economy.*

There is a consensus between the financial elite, neoclassical economists and the political classes in most countries that neoliberal policies will create global prosperity. So entrenched is their position that this view determines the policies of the international agencies (IMF, World Bank and WTO), and through them dictates the functioning of the global economy. Makwana, however, concludes that while a few people and large corporations have become extremely wealthy, neoliberal policies have been unable to benefit those living in extreme poverty or to address the growing levels of global inequality.

Teddy Goldsmith in an article "Poverty – The Child of Progress" (The Ecologist July/August 2001) agrees with Makwana. In his article he seeks to refute the claim that economic development utilizing neoliberal policy will eradicate poverty. He points out the near universal acceptance of this irrational dogma: *Economic development, in spite of its devastating effects on societies and the environment, remains the overriding goal of international agencies, national governments, and the transnational corporations that are of course its main promoters and beneficiaries. This is justified on the grounds that only development, and of course the global free trade that fuels it today, can eradicate poverty. Hardly anyone in a position of authority today seems willing to question this thesis, even though it is backed by neither any empirical nor any serious theoretical evidence.* After presenting a long list of statistics showing the reverse to be true – that poverty has worsened under economic development – Goldsmith concludes: *To reasonable people, these facts should be enough to discredit the dogma that development eradicates poverty. But for the promoters of development it merely indicates that it has not proceeded fast enough.*

Goldsmith then identifies the flaw in the development-eradicates-poverty theory: *By identifying poverty in purely monetary terms, it is assumed that money has always been, and always must be a prerequisite for satisfying real needs. This is simply not true.* He then describes the traditional non-monetary fulfilling of needs within the family and community and declares that: *Development changes all this. It is above all the gradual dis-embedding from their social context of these functions and their monetization, and takeover by corporations. As a result, a large section of society no longer has access to the money needed to pay for food, health care, and other now monetized benefits.*

We have been trained to believe that all pre-industrial people who lived in non-money economies were poor – but this is not true. Early travelers always noted how healthy and well fed were the traditional people whom they visited. After noting many examples, Goldsmith concludes: *In other words, tribal and other traditional people did not require economic development and the money it provides in order to be healthy and well fed.*

Goldsmith argues that in order to be successful, development must *create* social deprivation: *The main reason why development must create this deprivation is that, as more and more of the key functions that have always been fulfilled by families and communities are assumed by corporations, these key social units will simply atrophy, like muscles that are no longer in use. People will thereby be deprived of the most caring and most dependable sources of security. The bulk of the people in the industrialized world do not realize this. They depend on personal investments, on their jobs, and on the unstable global economy we have created. Jobs are increasingly precarious, while at the same time the welfare state, in order to reduce costs to industry, is being systematically dismantled. As this process occurs, vast numbers of people, increasingly deprived of family and community support, will find themselves deprived of virtually any form of security and will thereby join the proliferating throngs of the poor and destitute.*

Besides depriving people of the security that family and community provide, what other effects has neoliberal policy had worldwide? Has it eradicated poverty? Even though a relatively few people have become extremely wealthy, neoliberal policy has been unable to benefit those living in extreme poverty who are most in need of financial aid. Statistics show over and over again that this is true. Likewise, neoliberalism has been unable to address growing levels of global inequality. Makwana cites statistics that demonstrate this, as well.

Makwana continues: *The shortcomings of neoliberal policy are also apparent in the well documented economic disasters suffered by countries in Latin America and South Asia in the 1990's. These countries were left with no choice but to follow the neoliberal model of privatization and deregulation, due to their financial problems and pressure from the IMF. However, these problems were avoided by* the countries that rejected foreign corporate control and the advice of the IMF and World Bank.

Makwawa alleges that the U.S. and the European Union (EU) are unwilling to take their own medicine. He states: *However, there are huge differences between the neoliberal dogma that the US and European Union dictate to the world and the policies that they themselves adopt. While fiercely advocating the removal of barriers to trade, investment and employment, the U.S. economy remains one of the most protected in the world. Industrial nations only reached their state of economic development by fiercely protecting their industries from foreign markets and investment.* Makwana argues: *For economic growth to benefit developing countries, the international community must be allowed to nurture their infant industries. Instead, economically dominant countries are "kicking away the ladder" to achieving development by imposing an ideology that suits their own economic needs.*

The US and UK also provide huge subsidies to many sectors of industry. These devastate small industries in developing countries, particularly farmers who cannot compete with the price of subsidized goods in international markets. Despite their neoliberal rhetoric, most "capitalist" countries have increased their levels of state intervention over the past 25 years, and the size of their government has increased. The requirement is to "do as I say, not as I do".

So who are the beneficiaries of neoliberal policy? Makwana asserts: *The mandate for economic growth is the perfect platform for corporations which, as a result, have grown rapidly in their economic activity, profitability, and political influence. Yet this very model is also the cause of the growing inequalities seen across the globe. The privatization of resources and profits by the few at the expense of the many, and the inability of the poorest people to afford market prices, are both likely causes.*

Economic globalization has proceeded in two phases: 1) the phase of nation-state control—***modern state capitalism***—from 1945 - 1971 and 2) the phase of corporate control—which has no official name (we are not supposed to be aware of who really is in control) but is characterized by ***neoliberal economic policy*** based on ***"free market"*** ideology—from 1971 up to the present. Modern state capitalism called for the regulation of international capital which enhanced economic growth and permitted the Global North governments to undertake social democratic policies. The prosperity generated by the war was broadly shared in the U.S. creating a large, vibrant middle class.

The large U.S. corporations seemed content for a time, but as citizens' expectations from government increased in the 1960's and economic competition from West Germany and Japan grew, the corporations moved to take control of government itself. They saw governmental intercession on behalf of citizens as wasteful and as a drain on corporate profits. Beginning in the early 1970's, corporations pushed for, and received deregulation of international capital. This enabled them to largely usurp the powers traditionally held by the nation-states. Thomas Berry in his book *The Great Work* states: *That the corporations are the dominate powers on the national, and now on the global scale, is clear.*

The role of the nation-states at this point is to enforce corporate domination while appearing to serve the needs of the people. In the U.S. this has been, and remains, a bipartisan effort. Very often this entails military force. Thomas Friedman, writing in the New York Times (3/10/99) expressed this very candidly: *The hidden hand of the market will never work without a hidden fist – McDonalds cannot flourish without McDonnell Douglas, designer of the F-15, and the hidden fist that keeps the world safe for Silicon Valley's technologies is called the U.S. Army, Air Force, Navy, and Marine Corps.*

FIGURE:

The Global North elite. This small group of people consists of those individuals who make up the ruling classes of the nations of the Global North. They are those powerful forces in industry, banking and commerce who *de facto* rule the world. These nations are the United States (in the position of leadership), Western Europe, and Japan. They operate through a variety of forums to pursue their common interests. Considering the vast amount of power they wield, they remain virtually invisible to the great majority of people. This is intentional since elite interests are diametrically opposed to those of ordinary people, both in the Global South and the Global North.

In the U.S. they are the people in positions of power, both public and private, who determine domestic and foreign policy. Since the 1930's, they have used the forum of the **U.S. Council on Foreign Relations (CFR)** — a meeting ground for powerful members of the U.S. corporate and foreign policy establishments — to further their objectives. What are these objectives?

Following World War II, the elite of the victorious Allied powers, under U.S. leadership, determined that the basis of the postwar world economy would be a capitalist system of economic globalization. This would require international cooperation of the ruling classes of the leading industrial nations. In response to this need, the **Bilderberg** was formed in May, 1954. The Bilderberg (named for the hotel in which its initial meeting was held) is an unofficial, low-key (secret) group of powerful U.S. and Western European corporate and government elites. This group played a significant role in advancing the **European Union** and in shaping a consensus among U.S. and European leaders on key issues facing Western-dominated transnational corporations.

Economic globalization, under U.S. domination, worked reasonably well into the 1960's, at least from the standpoint of the rich industrialized nations. Following World War II, the top priority had been to rebuild the infrastructures and economies of Western Europe and Japan so that they could assume their roles as regional "managers" in the system and serve as markets for U.S. industrial production. Eventually, as their economies became stronger, West Germany and Japan challenged U.S. hegemony.

In 1971, President Nixon unilaterally introduced protectionist measures to benefit U.S. industries. The specter of trade wars, or worse, and the need for a forum with a more formal structure than the Bilderberg that would also include the Japanese led to the formation in 1973 of the **Trilateral Commission (TC).** Members of the TC describe themselves as "a group of concerned private citizens". Their purpose is to engineer an enduring partnership among the ruling classes of the member countries in order to safeguard the interests of Western capitalism. It foresees the eventual inclusion of the ruling classes of the "drop-out" nations — the Soviet Union, Eastern Europe, and China. Its like-minded members are drawn from international business and banking, government, academia, the media, and conservative labor.

The influence of the TC was felt in the 1976 election of Jimmy Carter, a commission member, to the presidency. Many of the key members of his administration were former members of both the TC and the Bilderberg. To illustrate its bipartisan nature, **Republican George Bush (senior)** and **Democrat Bill Clinton** were both commission members and promoted remarkably similar economic policies. Many members of Clinton's cabinet and other appointees are former commission members. (A person may not simultaneously hold a public office and be a member of the TC.) Its influence continues to be felt in other ways as one of its committees (the Preparatory) sets the agenda for the annual economic summits of the major industrialized nations (the Group of Seven). Its influence over IMF and World Bank policy is also considerable since TC recommendations are routinely adopted due to the weighted voting procedures in favor of the TC nations.

While major policy decisions are made by a select few within the CFR, the Bilderberg, and the TC, there are numerous organizations, national and international, which can be depended upon to support and implement these top-level decisions. They vary in their functions: some act primarily as lobbyists such as the **U.S. Chamber of Commerce** and the **American Farm Bureau Federation**. Although they claim to represent the interests of small business people and family farmers they, in reality, represent the interests of large corporations and agribusiness, respectively.

Other organizations exist for a specific purpose such as the **World Business Council for Sustainable Development** whose purpose is to preempt binding international agreements for environmental protection and **USA*Engage** which promotes the deregulation of international trade. Other organizations exist to extend credit to corporations such as the **U.S. Export-Import Bank** while others also provide guarantees and insurance such as the **U.S. Overseas Investment Corporation**. The most visible international organization, the **United Nations** (UN), established the **UN Commission on Trade and Development**. Its main purpose, working closely with the **International Chamber of Commerce**, is to stimulate corporate investment in the Global South. Not surprisingly, UN "peace keeping" missions favor U.S. and European corporate interests.

Other organizations, commonly called *think tanks*, produce literature with pro-corporate, oftentimes, conservative bias to be used by the media and government officials. These include: the **Brookings Institution**, the **Hoover Institution**, the **American Enterprise Institute**, the **Hudson Institute**, the **Heritage Foundation**, and the **Cato Institute**. They are funded by major corporations and wealthy individuals. Although there are think tanks with an opposing viewpoint, such as the **Institute for Policy Studies** and the **International Forum on Globalization**, they are poorly funded and are shunned by the corporate-owned mass media.

However, all these advantages were not enough for the ultra-rich in the U.S. The **Libertarian Party** was formed in 1971 in response to the growing demands, and the success of, citizen movements. In her book, *Democracy in Chains*, Nancy MacLain explains: *It's [the Libertarian Party's] founders sought a world in which liberty was preserved by the total absence of government coercion in any form. That entailed the end of public education, Social Security, Medicare, the U.S. Postal Service, minimum wage laws, prohibitions against child labor, foreign aid, the Environmental Protection Agency, prosecution for drug use or voluntary prostitution, and, in time, the end of taxes and government regulations of any kind.*

The Libertarian Party's attempt at electoral politics proved disappointing. In the 1980 presidential election, the ticket of Ed Clark for president and David Koch for vice president received only 1% of the vote, despite Koch himself contributing two million dollars to the campaign.

Realizing that the general public would never be able to see the "harm" in government largesse (the loss of "economic liberty", i.e. the ability to amass a fortune in the capitalist economy), the libertarians knew that a stealth policy would be necessary to enact their agenda. This effort was led by billionaire brothers **Charles and David Koch**. The Kochs have been holding secret, invitation-only meetings of wealthy conservative donors twice-yearly since 2003. However, after the election of **Barack Obama** in 2008, their fear of what his administration portended sent shock waves through their January 2009 meeting. Something had to be done.

In her book, *Dark Money*, Jane Mayer elaborates: *To this end, the Kochs waged a long and remarkable battle of ideas. They subsidized networks of seemingly unconnected think tanks and academic programs and spawned advocacy groups to make their arguments in the political debate. They hired lobbyists to push their interests in Congress and operatives to create synthetic grassroots groups to give their movement political momentum on the ground. In addition, they financed legal groups and judicial junkets to press their cases in the courts. Eventually, they added to this a private political machine that rivaled and threatened to subsume, the Republican Party. Much of this activism was cloaked in secrecy and presented as philanthropy [thus, tax-deductible] leaving almost no money trail that the public could trace. But, cumulatively it formed, as one of their operatives boasted in 2015, a "fully integrated network".*

Mayer continues: *The Kochs were unusually single-minded, but they were not alone. They were among a small, rarefied group of hugely wealthy, archconservative families that for decades poured money, often with little public disclosure, into influencing how Americans thought and voted. Their efforts began in earnest during the second half of the twentieth century. In addition to the Kochs, this group included Richard Mellon Scaife, an heir to the Mellon banking and Gulf Oil fortunes; Harry and Lynde Bradley, Midwesterners enriched by defense contracts; John M. Olin, a chemical and munitions company titan; the Coors brewing family of Colorado; and the DeVos family of Michigan, founders of the Amway marketing empire. Each was different, but together they formed a new generation of philanthropists, bent on using billions of dollars from their private foundations to alter the direction of American politics.*

The dust jacket blurb for MacLain's book, *Democracy in Chains*, opines: *Without [libertarian economist James M.] Buchanan's ideas and Koch's money, the libertarian cause would not have succeeded in its stealth takeover of the Republican Party as a delivery mechanism. Mike Pence's rise puts a longtime loyalist in the White House, backed by a phalanx of fighters in the House, the Senate, a majority of state governments, and many courts across the country. Their agenda includes measures calculated to kill off unions, keep millions of citizens from voting, privatize everything from schools to highways to Medicare and Social Security, stop any action on climate change – and transform the legal system and amend the Constitution to lock all of this in place permanently.*

MESSAGE IN SPEECH BALLOON AND "CONFIDENTIAL" STAMP:

While loudly proclaiming the supposed benefits of economic globalization, the method used to accomplish it (the pillars supporting the glass) are not for public consumption. Also, the extreme inequality in global wealth and the reason it exists are not to be exposed. Nor is the fact that this version of economic globalization that utilizes neoliberal policy would retain, if not further, global inequality.

The version of economic globalization championed by the United States following World War II was to be a capitalist system. The next lesson, not only looks at the economic system of capitalism, but also at the negative effects capitalism has had on the environment and on plant and animal species in the form of climate change and species extinction.

LESSON 3:
CAPITALISM AND CLIMATE CHANGE/ SPECIES EXTINCTION
DISCUSSION QUESTIONS

1. Have you ever questioned why all the profit should go to the owners? Or do you think it should?

2. What are the alternatives to capitalism? Or aren't there any?

3. Do you recall your parents or grandparents telling any stories about the Great Depression?

4. Why has consumption become such a dominant trend in the U.S.?

5. Do you see a connection between capitalism and climate change? Or is there none?

6. Why has the government been so resistant to addressing climate change?

7. Why is capitalism so fixated on economic growth?

OTHER POINTS OF DISCUSSION

Nowhere are the failings of profit-driven capitalism more apparent than in the actions of oil giant Exxon's decision to fund "climate denial". Despite its efforts for nearly two decades to raise doubts about the science of climate change, newly discovered company documents show that as early as 1977, Exxon research scientists warned company executives that carbon dioxide was increasing in the atmosphere and that the burning of fossil fuels was to blame.

The internal records are detailed in a new investigation published Wednesday by *InsideClimate News*, a Pulitzer Prize-winning news organization covering energy and the environment. The investigation found that long before global warming emerged as an issue on the national agenda, Exxon formed an internal brain trust that spent more than a decade trying to understand the impact of rising CO_2 levels in the atmosphere — even launching a supertanker with custom-made instruments to sample and understand whether the oceans could absorb the rising atmospheric CO_2 levels.

In 1978, the Exxon researchers warned that a doubling of CO_2 levels in the atmosphere would increase average global temperatures by 2 to 3 degrees Celsius and would have a major impact on the company's core business. "Present thinking holds that man has a time window of five to ten years before the need for hard decisions regarding changes in energy strategies might become critical," one scientist wrote in an internal document. The warnings would later grow more urgent. In a 1982 document marked "not to be distributed externally," the company's environmental affairs office wrote that preventing global warming would require sharp cuts in fossil fuel use. Failure to do so, the document said, could result in "some potentially catastrophic events" that "might not be reversible".

But in the mid-1980s, collapsing oil prices, among other pressures, pushed Exxon to change course, according to the InsideClimate News investigation, widening a gulf between its research arm and the company's executive suite. The report notes that by the 1990's: "Exxon helped to found and lead the Global Climate Coalition, an alliance of some of the world's largest companies seeking to halt government efforts to curb fossil fuel emissions. Exxon used the American Petroleum Institute, right-wing think tanks, campaign contributions and its own lobbying to push a narrative that climate science was too uncertain to necessitate cuts in fossil fuel emissions".

While it's impossible to know where the climate change debate would be today without Exxon's early decision to shift course on the science, the about-face was a lost opportunity in the overall effort to slow the rise of CO_2 emissions, according to one climate researcher interviewed by *InsideClimate News*. "All it would have taken is for one prominent fossil fuel CEO to know this was about more than just shareholder profits, and a question about our legacy," said Michael Mann, the director of the Earth System Science Center at Pennsylvania State University. "But now because of the cost of inaction — what I call the 'procrastination penalty' — we face a more uphill battle."

This essay is excerpted from an article by Jason M. Breslow entitled "Investigation Finds Exxon Ignored Its Own Early Climate Change Warnings" (9/16/15).

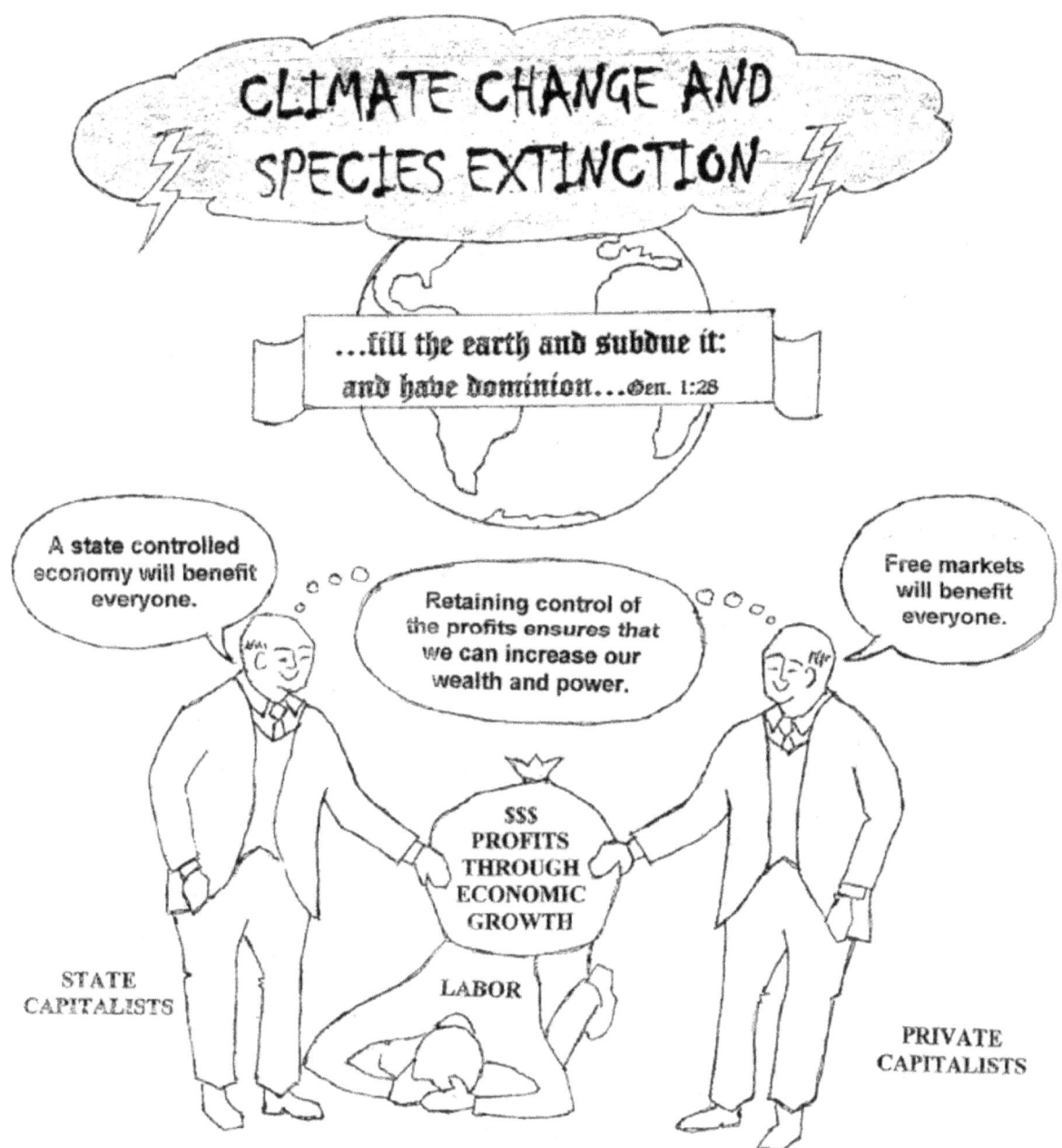

LESSON 3: CAPITALISM AND CLIMATE CHANGE / SPECIES EXTINCTION

THREE FIGURES:

The relationship between the capitalist owners and the labor force. There is a class relationship between the owners and the workers. The owners supply the means of production and the workers sell their labor to produce a product. The profit created in this process belongs solely to the owners.

FIGURE ON LEFT AND SPEECH BALLOON:

The state capitalists. Their message to the public is that the state can best regulate the economy to everyone's benefit. This group is comprised primarily of Democrats and Keynesian economists.

FIGURE ON RIGHT AND SPEECH BALLOON:

The private capitalists. Their message to the public is that an unfettered Free Market can best regulate the economy to everyone's benefit. This group is comprised primarily of Republicans and economists who follow the lead of Milton Friedman.

CENTRAL FIGURE:

The labor force.

THE CAPITALIST OWNERS HAVE THEIR HANDS ON THE BAG OF PROITS WHICH WEIGHS DOWN THE LABOR FORCE:

The capitalist owners decide how the profits will be used. They can be used to further oppress the labor force

THE STATE CAPITALISTS' AND THE PRIVATE CAPITALISTS' SHARED THOUGHT BALLOON:

The primary objective of the capitalist class is to retain their control of the profits produced by the capitalist system. They view profit as a means for personal enrichment and as a path to greater power which can lead to even greater profit.

BANNER SUPERIMPOSED ON THE EARTH:

The Western worldview of progress rigorously promotes the notion that the earth and its resources are at the disposal of and for the benefit of the human race. This view has Western religious sanction and popular acceptance in the Western culture and is essential to capitalism's demand for an ever-growing economy. Many indigenous and non-Western cultures strongly oppose this view and see care of the earth as a sacred duty.

OMINOUS CLOUD HANGS OVER THE EARTH:

The warming of the earth, primarily by the burning of fossil fuels and the practice of animal husbandry, is having serious consequences leading to climate change and species extinc-

LESSON 3: CAPITALISM AND CLIMATE CHANGE / SPECIES EXTINCTION

tion. Capitalism and the Western worldview of progress both see consumption as desirable, and are, therefore, in direct conflict with the need to control greenhouse emissions, a major cause of climate change. The demand of capitalism for ever greater economic growth is unsustainable on a planet with finite resources. Species extinction has happened at an accelerated rate ever since human beings populated the earth. However, it is currently increasing exponentially largely due to habitat loss and the effects of a warming planet, both due to human activity. The effects of climate change and species extinction are threatening life as we know it on this planet.

THREE FIGURES: The relationship between the capitalist owners and the labor force. There is a class relationship between the owners and the workers. The owners supply the means of production and the workers sell their labor to produce a product. The profit created in this process belongs solely to the owners.

Richard D. Wolff in his book *Capitalism Hits the Fan* explains capitalism and the relationship between owners and workers in this way: *"[C]apitalism refers to the system of production in which a relatively large group of people (productive laborers) sell their capacity to work to a relatively small group of different people (capitalist employers) for an agreed payment. The capitalist employers provide the "means of production" (tools, equipment, and raw material) for the productive laborers to work with and on. There are two key aspects of the relationship between capitalists and productive laborers. First, what the laborers produce belongs instantly and automatically to the capitalist who sells it. Second, the revenue from that sale must exceed what the capitalist paid for the means of production and to the productive laborers. The excess is the surplus, the fund from which the capitalist distributes portions to reproduce capitalism as a system (portions including interest to creditors, dividends to shareholders, budgets to managers and advertisers, profits retained for enterprise growth, etc.).*

FIGURE ON LEFT AND SPEECH BALLOON:

The state capitalists. Their message to the public is that the state can best regulate the economy to everyone's benefit. This group is comprised primarily of Democrats and Keynesian economists.

FIGURE ON RIGHT AND SPEECH BALLOON:

The private capitalists. Their message to the public is that an unfettered Free Market can best regulate the economy to everyone's benefit. This group is comprised primarily of Republicans and economists who follow the lead of Milton Friedman.

CENTRAL FIGURE:

The labor force.

THE CAPITALIST OWNERS HAVE THEIR HANDS ON THE BAG OF PROFITS WHICH WEIGHS DOWN THE LAROR FORCE:

The capitalist owners decide how the profits will be used. They can be used to further oppress the labor force.

THE STATE CAPITALISTS' AND THE PRIVATE CAPITALISTS' SHARED THOUGHT

LESSON 3: CAPITALISM AND CLIMATE CHANGE / SPECIES EXTINCTION

BALLOON:

The primary objective of the capitalist class is to retain their control of the profits. They view profit as a means for personal enrichment and as a path to greater power which can lead to even greater profit. If needed, profit can be used to keep the populous under control.

How do the two forms of capitalism relate to each other? Wolff explains: *Throughout its history and across geography, capitalism has swung back and forth between private and state forms. The former reduces while the latter enlarges the state's intervention in the economy. The economic events that precipitate swings (in both directions) have been various mixes of recession and widening inequality. Political oscillations have paralleled the economic. Often the party or faction losing power is the one most closely associated with the kind of capitalism being displaced, while the ascendant party or faction champions the other kind.*

The Great Depression of 1929 yielded such a victory to FDR's New Deal and it's Keynesian economics [the state capitalists]. The Republicans went to work to undo FDR and his legacy, while Milton Friedman and his ilk went to work to undo Keynesian economics [the private capitalists]. Neither succeeded until the US economy experienced a meltdown in the 1970's. Severe economic problems throughout the 1970's strengthened the Republicans sufficiently to allow them to undo and reverse the New Deal: Reagan's "revolution". With the next panic, set off by the US stock market's burst bubble early in 2000, the debate revived. Paul Krugman and his ilk could then revive the "state intervention is necessary" song and dance.

However, the similarity between the two forms of capitalism is far greater than their differences. *Wolff explains: What both kinds of capitalism have in common – what makes them alternative kinds of one system – is the shared structure of the surplus-yielding employer/employee relationship.* **The profits must remain in the hands of the capitalist class.**

But why shouldn't the workers receive and distribute the surpluses that they produce? Why shouldn't they be their own bosses, eliminating the class difference and antagonism between the owners and the workers? Liberals and even most radicals over the last century have excluded these revolutionary demands in favor of winning incremental reforms such as reducing unemployment, raising wages, improving working conditions, reducing racial and gender discrimination, improving educational opportunities, healthcare and so on. They see revolutionary change as a dangerous delusion. Ironically, any reforms that are made can be undone much more easily than they were won as the wealth of the owning class continues to outpace that of the working class.

What caused the economic meltdown beginning in the 1970's? Wolff explains: *A big part of the answer lies in the unique history of US capitalism. From 1820 to 1970, over every decade, average real wages rose, enabling a rising standard of consumption. An unspoken historic deal defined US capitalism for those 150 years. Capitalists paid rising wages to enable rising working class consumption; the workers had to provide rising work effort, rising profitability, and thus the even faster rise of profits.*

As a result of this dynamic—higher wages for the workers but even greater profits for the owners—a fundamentally unequal society emerged with the working class falling ever farther behind the capitalist owning class. By the 1970's the owners no longer needed this arrangement and abandoned it in favor of out-sourcing jobs to low-wage countries and letting the wages of U.S. workers stagnate. Automation, new technologies and the weakening of labor unions also played a role in this change.

But 150 years of rising levels of consumption had had their effect. *The idea [had] settled into US culture that consumption was the proper goal of work and the measure of personal worth, of one's "success" in life. Consumerism's deep roots in the psyche of US workers explains their reactions when real wages stopped rising in the 1970's and since. They simply kept on buying more commodities. To pay for them, workers took on more hours of labor and borrowed vast sums. Worker exhaustion rose accordingly, likewise the number of family members sent out to work. Anxiety intensified over frightening family debt levels. In this situation, the current scandal of sub-prime mortgages was a predictable disaster waiting to happen.*

But, the most damaging feature of capitalism may well be its undermining of democracy through its promotion of "free market" ideology. In his book *The New Human Rights Movement: Reinventing the Economy to End Oppression* Peter Joseph explains: *The molding of modern day capitalism over time was inevitable as more complex labor roles and technology unfolded. In this, the once obvious social and undemocratic power imbalances of early societies slowly became cloaked by the idealism of the "free market". Unlike in earlier eras, which featured intolerant government monarchs, abject slavery, and other more primitive forms of dictatorial power and direct oppression, this new structure provided the illusion of democratic participation, rights, and freedom by structurally submerging social dominance within the mass competitive act of "free trade". The beauty of this means of social domination is that it facilitates the pretense that totalitarianism doesn't exist. Kings and regimes no longer wield total control over the lives of their subjects. Rather, power and wealth remain concentrated by way of a process of competitive advantage in the market – a process that is provably undemocratic and structurally rigged to favor a small, undefined, transient minority in the same basic manner (yet obscured) by which a monarch exerted control.*

Joseph continues: *In effect, the ethic of trade and markets has become synonymous with democracy and freedom. Any talk of government directly assisting a population in an organized, streamlined capacity – efficiently using resources in a way only larger-order design and organization can achieve – is derailed derisively as "socialist" interference with "market freedom". This process of maturation of capitalism has sanctified or normalized the idea that some should be very rich and powerful and most should be very poor and impotent. This ethos is preserved by the mythology that any other way can only be "anti-freedom".*

Capitalism can be seen as the latest stage of an ethic that rewards the powerful and wealthy at the expense of everyone else. It is widely accepted by experts in the field that for 99% of human existence people lived in hunter-gatherer societies. These societies were egalitarian and consumption varied little across their members. As seen in Lesson 1, this ethic also prevailed in the settled communities that practiced a partnership model of society. However, these defenseless societies were systematically decimated by pastoralist invaders who practiced a dominator model of society that justified and rewarded competition, self-interest, hierarchy, inequality, and oppression.

Joseph elaborates: *"Since that time [the Neolithic era], people have been divided into two groups: those who toil for little reward and have little social or political power and those who maintain vastly disproportionate wealth, social influence, and political power, generally at the expense of those toiling. We see this broad socioeconomic duality across all historical social systems, such as abject slaves and ruling monarch-deities in ancient Egypt; vassals and lords in medieval feudal societies; handicraft merchants and state monopolists of mercantilism; and workers and owners in contemporary capitalism. Regardless of the era, economic and social inequality has persisted for millennia. While terms for the privileged or elite "in-group" have changed over time, god-kings to aristocracy to bourgeoisie to today's ownership or investment class, the systemic framework that has assured one group will be superior to another has not changed.*

Not only is capitalism undermining democracy and creating extreme inequality between and within countries, it is a threat to the future of the planet itself with its finite resources and delicate eco-systems. The very nature of capitalism and its "profit motive" demands that the economy must "grow". Ever greater economic growth requires more resources and more energy.

How is economic growth accomplished? Michael Parenti in his book *Democracy for the Few* explains: *Capitalists like to say they are "putting their money to work," but money as such cannot create more wealth. What capitalists really mean is that they are putting more human labor power to work, paying workers less in wages than they produce in value, thereby siphoning off more profit for themselves. That's how money "grows".* Parenti continues: *Under capitalism, the ultimate purpose of work is not to produce goods and services but to make money for the investor. As David Roderick, the president of U.S. Steel (now USX) put it: "United States Steel Corporation is not in the business of making steel. We're in the business of making profits."*

This relentless pursuit of profit results from something more than just greed – although there is enough of that. Under capitalism, enterprises must expand in order to survive. To stand still amidst growth is to decline, not only relatively but absolutely. A slow-growth firm is less able to move into new markets, hold onto old ones, command investment capital, and control suppliers. A decline in the rate of production eventually cuts into profits and leads to a company's decline. Even the biggest corporations, enjoying a relatively secure oligopolistic control over markets, are beset by a ceaseless drive to expand, to find new ways of making money. Ultimately, the only certainty, even for the giants, is uncertainty. Larger size, greater reserves, and better organizational control might bring security were it not that all other companies are pursuing these same goals. So survival can never be taken for granted.

Capitalism's values are also expressed in how productivity is measured – **gross national product (GNP)**. Parenti explains: *Important nonmarket services like housework and child rearing go uncounted, while many things of negative social value are tabulated. Thus, highway accidents, which lead to increased insurance, hospital, and police costs, add quite a bit to the GNP but take a lot out of life.*

Parenti insists: *The **human** value of productivity rests in its social purpose. Is the purpose to plunder the environment without regard to ecological needs, fabricate endless consumer desires, produce shoddy goods designed to wear out quickly, create wasteful forms of consumption, pander to snobbism and acquisitiveness, squeeze as much compulsive toil as possible out of workers while paying them as little as possible, create artificial scarcities in order to jack up prices – all in order to grab as big a profit as one can? Or, is productivity geared to serve essential needs first and superfluous wants last, to care for the natural environment and the health and safety of citizens and workers? Is it organized to maximize the capabilities, responsibilities, and participation of its people?*

Parenti concludes: *Capitalist productivity-for-profit gives little consideration to the latter set of goals. What is called productivity, as measured quantitatively, may actually represent a decline in the*

LESSON 3: CAPITALISM AND CLIMATE CHANGE / SPECIES EXTINCTION

quality of life – for example, the relationship between the increasing quantity of automotive and industrial usage and the decreasing quality of our environment. Under capitalism, there is a glut of nonessential goods and services for those with money and a shortage of essential ones for those without money. Stores groan with unsold items while millions of people are ill-housed and ill-fed.

But aren't useful goods produced in the capitalist process of economic growth? Originally, capitalists focused on products useful to life such as food and clothing with cloth being the first major commodity of the capitalist market. But since maximal profit is the goal of capitalism, the capitalist owners turned to nonessential items such as junk food and automobiles that would produce higher profits. Then they proceeded to turn these nonessential wants into needs.

Most people today would consider an automobile a need, not a nonessential want, but it didn't have to be that way. Using transportation as an example, Parenti explains how capitalists turned a nonessential want into a need: *Earlier in this century* [the twentieth century] *the transporting of passengers and goods was done mostly by electric car and railroad. One mass-transit railway car can do the work of fifty automobiles, and railroads consume one-sixth the energy of trucks to transport goods. But these very efficiencies are what made railroads so* **undesirable** *to the oil and auto industries. For over a half-century, their response has been to undermine the nation's rail and electric-bus systems.*

Using dummy corporations, these industries bought up the quiet, non-polluting street car systems, junked them, and replaced them with buses. When they realized that more profit could be made from automobile use, they increased bus fares, eliminated routes, and in general, made service so undependable that people had no choice, in many cases, but to travel by car. The oil and automobile industries demanded that the government construct a national highway system at public expense, which was done. The railway system was likewise sabotaged.

By 1955, 88 percent of the nation's electric-streetcar network had been eliminated by collaborators such as General Motors, Standard Oil, Greyhound, and Firestone. Given the absence of alternative modes of transportation, people became dependent on the automobile as a way of life so that their need for cars is often as real as their need for jobs – and mass transit devolves into "mess transit". Parenti points out the logic of this madness: *But as worldwide car usage grows so do the profits of the oil, auto, trucking, tire, cement, construction, and motel businesses.*

Capitalism does not recognize a distinction between profit gained from a socially beneficial product and that gained from a socially destructive one. John McMurtry in his book The Cancer Stage of Capitalism uses the arms industry as the prime example: *The primary form* [of life destruction] *is to invest in producing and selling lethal weapons. These are researched, designed, and produced so as to destroy human life and its infrastructural supports with the maximal efficiency which the physical, biological, and engineering sciences can achieve. Most public research money in the world's richest nation* [the United States] *is assigned to this form of research, which is then appropriated by private corporations to produce, sell, and export increasingly expensive and deadly weapons for profit.*

Although the production and use of lethal weapons have a long history, the process was escalated after the Russian Revolution of 1917 in order to rule out the possibility that an alternative economic system to capitalism would develop. The arms industry has become the most profitable industry in the world. McMurtry lists the reason that capitalism favors the production of lethal weapons:

1) *Their uniquely high value-added price, whether sold as an overall weapons system or as an individual component, accessory, replacement, or part (for example, $26 billion for the first five years of research and development of the U.S. "Stars Wars" program, or $7,417.00 spent by the U.S. government to General Electric for two one-cent pins);*

2) *Their especially rapid rate of obsolescence and turnover, which follows from both arms-race market conditions and from rapid destruction of these commodities by their use;*

3) *The monopoly or semi-monopoly position of armaments manufacturers;*

4) *The large-scale and secure capital financing of military research, production and cost-additions; a funding which is ensured by coercive state mechanisms of public taxation, resource allocation, and national-debt imposition, and which is available to no other system of commodity production.*

International moneylenders thrive on the arms industry since most weapons purchases are financed through the acquisition of long-term debt. Weapons of terror and destruction are then often required to compel indebted nations to pay their multiplying debt load. The apparent "madness of the arms race" and the "insanity of the military institution" (while surely true from an ethic that values life) are, in fact, perfectly rational from the standpoint of capitalism with its purpose of returning maximal profits to corporate shareholders and investors regardless of the consequences to human life and the environment.

This also explains how stories of humanity's natural aggression and love of war can continue to be believed in as long as the real reason for weapons proliferation—the corporate profits they generate—remains hidden from public view. It is not surprising that the George W. Bush administration, with strong bipartisan support, responded to the attacks on the twin towers of the World Trade Center and the Pentagon on September 11, 2001 by declaring a "war on terrorism".

Arhundhati Roy, in an article that appeared in the September 29, 2001 London Guardian, points out the illogic of a military response: *What we're witnessing here is the spectacle of the world's most powerful country reacting reflexively, angrily, for an old instinct to fight a new kind of war. Suddenly, when it comes to defending itself, America's streamlined warships, cruise missiles, and F-16 jets look like obsolete, lumbering things. As deterrence, its arsenal of nuclear bombs is no longer worth its weight in scrap. Box-cutters, penknives, and cold anger are the weapons with which the wars of the new century will be waged. Anger is the lock pick. It slips through customs unnoticed. It doesn't show up in the baggage checks.*

In his book, McMurtry describes the downward progression of capitalism's selection process from useful goods, to nonessential goods, to life-destroying goods. However, what he has labeled the ***cancer stage of capitalism*** is when no goods at all are produced and money is used solely to produce more money. The most common form of this practice is ***compound-interest debt.*** It is conservatively estimated that 40 times more money value is commanded this way, daily, than from all expenditures on goods and services combined. The inner logic of the capitalist market system is not to solve the Global South debt crisis, but to ***keep*** the Global South

LESSON 3: CAPITALISM AND CLIMATE CHANGE / SPECIES EXTINCTION

nations indebted on a permanent and rising basis, while in the process, dismantling social sectors.

McMurtry argues, however, that this is not really a crisis of capitalism, but of a nonfunctioning deformation of it. Global South debt owed to Global North lenders—as are all money-to-more-money sequences that produce no goods—is a cancerous mutation of capitalism. Like all cancers, the mutant forms of uncontrolled, disoriented self-multiplication (money-to-more-money sequences) have no committed function to their life-host, which in this case, is the rest of humanity and the environment which sustains life. They draw the life-sustaining sustenance from the life-host, but give nothing in return. And like all parasites, if not destroyed in time to save the host, it will eventually perish along with the life-host it has invaded. So money producing only more money—*usury*—is the final and most destructive assault of capitalism—a system, which by its very nature and in all its forms, benefits the few at the expense of the many.

So, not only does capitalism lead to ever greater inequality, it is a threat to the health of the planet as it plunders its finite resources and disregards real human needs in favor of much that is detrimental to human life.

BANNER SUPERIMPOSED ON THE EARTH:

The Western worldview of progress rigorously promotes the notion that the earth and its resources are at the disposal of and for the benefit of the human race. This view has Western religious sanction and popular acceptance in the Western culture and is essential to capitalism's demand for an ever-growing economy. Many indigenous and non-Western religions and cultures strongly oppose this view and see care of the earth as a sacred duty. A further concern is how capitalist values are implicated in global warming and climate change, as well as species extinction.

OMINOUS CLOUD HANGS OVER THE EARTH:

The warming of the earth, primarily by the burning of fossil fuels and the practice of animal husbandry, is having serious consequences leading to climate change and species extinction. Capitalism and the Western worldview of progress both see consumption as desirable, and are, therefore, in direct conflict with the need to control greenhouse emissions, a major cause of climate change. The demand of capitalism for ever greater economic growth is unsustainable on a planet with finite resources. Species extinction has happened at an accelerated rate ever since human beings populated the earth. However, it is currently increasing exponentially largely due to habitat loss and the effects of a warming planet, both due to human activity. The effects of climate change and species extinction are threatening life as we know it on this planet.

In an article entitled "What is Climate Change?" (1/24/16) Jenn Savedge asks: *What exactly is climate change and how is it having such a major effect on the planet? The term, "climate change," refers to the recent statistical phenomenon that shows that the Earth is warming at a rate that is unlike anything scientists have seen for thousands of years. While there are some skeptics, 97 percent of climate scientists agree that climate change is happening. Not only that, but these scientists also agree that these warming trends have been and continue to be caused by human activities.*

48 LESSON 3: CAPITALISM AND CLIMATE CHANGE / SPECIES EXTINCTION

Savedge then asks: **What causes climate change?** *The primary cause of climate change is the enhanced "greenhouse effect" that is caused when human activities – such as burning fossil fuels, clearing land for agriculture, and other industrial activities – releases gases into the environment. The gases, namely carbon dioxide, methane, chlorofluorocarbons, and nitrous oxide are called "greenhouse gases" because they absorb heat from the sun and trap it in the Earth's atmosphere. But when too many of these gases are released, they build up in the atmosphere, warming the planet beyond levels that have sustained living creatures for centuries.*

According to the website of the Union of Concerned Scientists: Global warming is already having significant and harmful effects on our communities, our health, and our climate. Sea level rise is accelerating. The number of large wildfires is growing. Dangerous heat waves are becoming more common. Extreme storm events are increasing in many areas. More severe droughts are occurring in others.

Their conclusion: *We must take immediate action to address global warming or these consequences will continue to intensify, grow ever more costly, and increasingly affect the entire planet – including you, your community, and your family. The good news is that we have the practical solutions at hand to dramatically reduce our carbon emissions, slow the pace of global warming, and pass on a healthier, safer world to future generations.*

So why isn't this happening? The fossil fuel industry is opposed to anything that would affect their profits. They are taking the lead in the "climate change denial" movement [see introductory essay]. A capitalist economic system demands this type of unprincipled behavior.

In addressing species extinction, which is also an assault on the natural world by capitalism, Ashley Dawson in his book *Extinction: A Radical History* explains: *Humanity lives amid, and is the cause of, a massive decimation of global biodiversity. From humble invertebrates like beetles and butterflies to various terrestrial vertebrate populations like bats and birds, species are going extinct in record numbers. Researchers generally agree that the current extinction rate is nothing short of catastrophic, clocking in between one thousand and ten thousand times the rate before human beings began to exert a significant pressure on the environment.*

The earth is losing about a hundred species a day. In addition to this tidal wave of extinction, which conservation biologists predict will eliminate up to 50 percent of currently existing animal and plant species, the abundance of species in local areas is declining precipitously, threatening the functioning of entire ecosystems. This mass extinction is thus an under-acknowledged form – and cause- of the contemporary environmental crisis. This wave [of extinction] *is predicted to be the worst catastrophe for life on Earth since the asteroid impact that destroyed the dinosaurs.*

The class system of capitalism has done untold harm both to workers and to the environment. For more information on the human and environmental effects of capitalism see Lesson 8. But capitalism itself is only part of the problem. In the next lesson we will see how the promoters of economic globalization use the corporate structure to further their advantage.

LESSON 4:
CORPORATIONS
DISCUSSION QUESTIONS

1. Should owners of a corporation be responsible for damages caused by the corporation?

2. What, if anything, is the relationship between corporate power and democracy?

3. Should the "natural person" status of corporations be revoked?

4. What are some alternatives to corporations that would better serve local communities and protect the environment?

5. What is your perception of regulatory agencies?

6. Previous to this study, were you aware of the "wealth bias" built into the U.S. Constitution?

7. Should corporations be allowed to exist only to provide a public service? Should other limitations be placed on corporations?

OTHER POINTS OF DISCUSSION

Is the corporate business structure per se the problem, or is it just a tool in the hands of people who can produce either helpful or harmful results? While many of the large, transnational corporations are being blamed for much of what is wrong in the world today, Sharon Thompson often relates a story about a different kind of corporation—one that proved to be a good neighbor and friend in a time of need.

Sharon and her husband, Gordon, own and operate a dairy farm southwest of Lakeville, MN. One chilly March morning, Sharon arrived home from a church meeting to find Gordon lying on the ground. She was greeted with these words: "Turn off the silo unloader and then get some help. I have a broken leg." The broken leg, caused by an accident with the bull, required hospitalization and surgery. Sharon, with the help of her six daughters and a brother-in-law, managed to keep things running relatively smoothly in Gordon's absence. That is, until one morning, following a wet, heavy snowfall during the night, a huge dip in the middle of the barn roof caught Sharon's attention.

She immediately went to the phone and called Dale "Skip" Fredrickson of Fredrickson Lumber & Construction, Inc. Dale and his wife are the corporate owners of a small lumber yard that specializes in the construction of pole buildings. The phone conversation went something like this:

"Good morning. Fredrickson Lumber. Skip speaking."

"Hi, Skip, this is Sharon Thompson. Say, I really have a problem here. Part of the barn roof buckled during the night. It must have been weak and the snow was just too much for it."

"I'd better have a look at it. I'll be right over."

"Thanks a lot, Skip. I really appreciate it."

"No problem."

Skip promptly arrived, sized up the job, jotted some figures on a pad of paper, and announced: "I'll be back in the morning with a crew." The work was completed and Sharon didn't think too much more about it until the bill arrived in the mail. The hand-written bill itemized the materials used, followed by the cost of each. The last item listed was "Labor". Under the expense column two words were written: "No Charge".

What is the difference between the Enron Corporation and Fredrickson Lumber & Construction, Inc.? When the collapse of Enron was imminent, the top officials chose to conceal that fact from their employees and the general public, allowing the officials to sell off their stock at inflated prices. The employees, not given that option, were left holding nearly worthless stock. Many employees not only lost their jobs, but their retirement income as well. In sharp contrast, Skip Fredrickson chose to forego some of his profit in order to help out a neighbor/customer. At what point does profit become more important than people? Is it when a corporation becomes so large and remote that employees are seen only as an additional expense and customers are seen only as consumers of a corporate product and no longer as people? It would seem so.

LESSON 4: CORPORATIONS

FIGURE OBSCURES "U.S. POST-WW II ECONOMIC PLAN":

The U.S. elite use legal means to carry out their plan for implementing economic globalization. However, it is necessary to keep their true objectives hidden from public view. One of the most effective tools in accomplishing their goals is corporations.

FIGURE HOLDS PLACARD CITING THE LEGAL BASIS OF CORPORATE POWER:

This includes a variety of methods.

By law the corporate business structure allows:

1. **Unlimited growth.** Corporations can raise vast amounts of financial capital. This allows them the potential for virtually unlimited growth. The sheer size of these relatively few giant corporations is part of the problem. They have enormous economic power that permits them to escape the discipline of the competitive market giving them substantial control over the prices charged for the goods they produce. Economic power also gives them political power.

2. **Limited liability.** A corporation has limited liability. The owners of a corporation are not liable for its debts beyond their investment or for any harm done by their company's business activities.

3. **Corporate Personhood Court Decision:** Corporations have *"natural person"* status under the law, allowing them to claim the rights guaranteed human persons in the *Bill of Rights*. This now includes making unlimited campaign contributions to political candidates due to the 2009 Citizens United Supreme Court decision.

4. **Regulatory Agency Laws:** Regulatory agencies are another method used by the U.S. elite to consolidate and increase their wealth and power. Most U.S. citizens believe that regulatory agencies were created to operate in the public's behalf to minimize harm done by corporations. This is not so.

5. **Property Rights Clauses of U.S. Constitution:** While greatly revered, this document institutionalized the dominance of large commercial interests over small businessmen, artisans and the general public. The U.S. elite use this Constitutional bias towards wealth to their own advantage.

MESSAGE IN SPEECH BALLOON OF FIGURE TRAMPLING ON PAPER THAT STATES: "CORPORATIONS SHOULD BE ALLOWED TO EXIST ONLY TO PROVIDE A PUBLIC SERVICE":

The original purpose of corporations "to provide a public service" has been thoroughly undermined by the U.S. elite. Through law and tradition the purpose has become "to maximize profits to shareholders." This change has had a very damaging effect on the democratic process in the U.S. as well as having devastating effects on the environment and the Global South poor.

LESSON 4: CORPORATIONS

FIGURE OBSCURES "U.S. POST-WW II ECONOMIC PLAN":

The U.S. elite use legal means to carry out their plans for implementing economic globalization. One of their most effective tools is corporations. However, it is necessary to keep their true objectives hidden from public view.

FIGURE HOLDS PLACARD CITING THE LEGAL BASIS OF CORPORATE POWER:

This involves a variety of methods. But first of all, what exactly is a corporation? How does it differ from other types of business organizations and why is this such an advantage to the U.S. elite? What is a corporation? A *corporation* is an organization recognized and created by law that allows people to associate together for a common purpose under a common name. It is a key economic institution, even though it is not the most prevalent form of business organization. In the U.S. a corporation must receive a charter from the government before it can be organized. This power is exercised mainly by the states. Business corporations are known as *joint-stock companies* because they are jointly owned by different persons who receive shares of stock in exchange for an investment of money in the venture. Most corporations are publicly-owned, that is, they are owned through shares held by private individuals, i.e. the public. Shares are traded in organized markets such as the *New York Stock Exchange.* The majority of corporations are small, differing little in their characteristics from other forms of businesses. Overall, corporations make up approximately 25 percent of all business firms in the U. S. This figure, however, drastically understates the real economic significance of the corporate business organization. In the current U.S. economy, a relative handful of corporate giants account for about half of all the goods and services produced in the nation. Corporations with assets in excess of $250 million number less than 1 percent of U.S. companies, but they dominate production and exchange in all parts of the economy—in manufacturing, transportation and utilities, mining, banking and insurance, and retail trade. Corporate mergers in the 19th century, in the 1920's, and after World War II, as well as modern technological developments, largely account for the appearance of corporate giants in these sectors of the economy. What advantages do corporations have that other business structures do not have?

By law, the corporate business structure allows:

1. **Unlimited growth.** Corporations can raise vast amounts of financial capital. This allows them the potential for virtually unlimited growth. The sheer size of these relatively few giant corporations is part of the problem. They have enormous economic power that permits then to escape the discipline of the competitive market giving them substantial control over the prices charged for the goods they produce. Economic power also gives them political power. The two major U.S. political parties are beholden to the giant corporations which fund the political campaigns of candidates of both parties who are then obligated to pursue a pro-corporate agenda.

2. **Limited liability.** A corporation has limited liability. The owners of a corporation are not liable for its debts beyond their investment or for any harm done by their company's business activities. Jim Hightower in his book *If the Gods Had Meant Us to Vote, They Would Have Given Us Candidates* explains: *The corporation is a legal shield, granting its owners an extraordinary protective privilege that no other business owners are allowed. Oh,*

did my company spill eleven million gallons of oil into Prince William Sound (Exxon), did it kill two thousand people in a chemical explosion in Bhopal, India (Union Carbide), did it defraud thousands of senior citizens who were persuaded to put money into bad securities (Prudential), did it dump cancer-causing PCB's into the Hudson River (General Electric)? So sorry, I'm sure, but that's none of my doing – the corporation did it.

How did corporations attain the power and privileges they now enjoy? What is their origin and history? Although the origin of corporations as a legal form can be traced back to Roman times, the voyages of exploration and discovery in the 16th and 17th centuries greatly stimulated the use of the corporate form of organization. Kalle Lasn and Tom Liacas in a magazine article "1600-1886 the Birth of the Corporate 'I'" (Adbusters, No. 31, Aug/Sept 00) explain how this process worked: *As North America was colonized, corporations like the Massachusetts Bay Company and the Hudson's Bay Company were there every step of the way. These early corporations were conceived as institutions serving the public interest. They were temporary structures granted the right to operate for a fixed period of time, with fixed capital, to achieve fixed goals.*

To lay claim to the whole of the New World, though, the British Crown needed huge amounts of capital. To encourage investment in such a large and risky enterprise, the Crown agreed to insulate investors from legal responsibility for the undertaking, beyond the amount of their investment. In other words, investors were not liable, in the last resort, for the debts of their company. That decision blew apart one of the bedrock principles of common law: individual responsibility. For the first time, business investors were privileged with limited liability.

However, what proved to be a beneficial arrangement for the European governments (expansion of their wealth and power by creating colonies that served both as sources of raw materials and as markets for exported goods) and the corporations they chartered (risk-free investments) proved to have the opposite effect for the colonists. Lasn and Liacas continue: *Colonials feared these chartered entities. They recognized the way British kings and their cronies used corporations as robotic arms to maintain their sovereignty and control over the affairs of the colonies. The American Revolution was in large part a revolt against what Thomas Jefferson called this "remote tyranny".*

The Declaration of Independence freed Americans not only from Britain but also from the control of British corporations, and for 100 years after the document's signing, Americans remained deeply suspicious of corporate power. The 200 or so corporations operating in the U.S. by the year 1800 were kept on short leashes. They weren't allowed to participate in the political process. They couldn't buy stock in other corporations. And if one of them acted improperly, the consequences were severe.

However, the concept that corporations were allowed to exist to provide a public service (such as digging a canal, building a bridge, constructing a road, or providing financial services) was soon to be eroded. President Thomas Jefferson's embargo of France and England from 1807 to 1809 and by the War of 1812 shut down trade with Europe. In order to supply the domestic market with the manufactured goods that previously had come from Europe, U.S. corporations were formed to amass the capital needed to build factories. These factories were not designed to fulfill a public service, but rather to create private wealth for the owners through the manufacture of consumer goods.

The simultaneous rise of capitalism as the predominant economic system, the Industrial Revolution which was fueled by the resources and slave labor of the European colonies and

LESSON 4: CORPORATIONS 55

the ability of corporations to amass huge amounts of money with limited liability in the pursuit of private profit proved to be a major turning point in U.S. and human history. Lasn and Liacas continue: *By the middle of the 19th century, the nation's commercial engine was humming, and corporations were becoming an indispensable part of business life. They pushed for and gained extended rights and freedoms in their charters. Then, in a series of landmark decisions, state legislatures, one after another, enacted "free incorporation laws" that gave corporations the right to engage in any kind of business they wanted. This was a crucial step in the evolution of the corporate form. Corporations were no longer limited to activities that served the public good, yet they continued to enjoy the extraordinary "limited liability" exemption from investor responsibility that they had historically obtained in the name of public service.*

During the Civil War, corporations bagged huge profits from procurement contracts. They took advantage of the chaos and corruption of the times to buy judges, legislatures, and even presidents. They forced amendments to laws that limited their profits and in hundreds of cases, won minor legal victories extending their rights and privileges. They had immense political clout. Civil society was reeling, unable to keep up. Then came **Santa Clara***, that pivotal 1886 decision, which gave corporations the final boost they needed - "natural person" status under the law. It was one of the greatest blunders in legal history, and it triggered the corporations' hundred-year march to global power.*

Corporate Personhood Court Decision: Corporations have "natural person" status under the law, allowing then to claim the rights guaranteed human persons in the **Bill of Rights**. What exactly does "natural person" status under the law mean? And what are the implications of it? Betsy Barnum, former AfD – MN member, explained the essence of **corporate personhood**: *There is growing awareness in the U.S. that corporations wield massively excessive power, which interferes with democracy and overshadows every realm of our lives. One of the ways in which corporations have been allowed to accumulate such immense power is through an 1886 federal court decision in California, upheld by the U.S. Supreme Court, that the 14th Amendment to the Constitution which guarantees individual rights to all* **persons** *applies not just to human persons, but also to corporations. The granting of personhood to corporations has led to their claiming of almost all the individual rights in the Bill of Rights, including free speech, due process, and equal protection. Through these means, almost everything a corporation does is legally defined as* **private property***, in some way protected by the* **Bill of Rights***.*

The concept of corporate personhood can be traced back to the 1886 Supreme Court case *Santa Clara v. Southern Pacific Railroad*. This case would test the "legal person" status of corporations. Surprisingly, the court refused to even hear it. Instead, they unanimously held: "We always thought it [the corporation] was a legal person." By the court's silence, corporations now had the same Constitutional rights as real people. What are some of the implications of this ruling? The *Corporate Personhood Resolution of the City of Point Arena, California* addresses this question: *How many people know that under U.S. law, corporations are persons? And that, as a result corporations have been able to amass ever greater power to influence democratic processes and restrain governmental regulation? For example:*

- *Do advocates for campaign finance reform know that corporations cannot be prevented from contributing money to political campaigns?* **Corporate personhood means that any restraints on campaign contributions represent an abridgment of corporate rights to free speech.** [This now includes making unlimited campaign contributions to political candidates due to the 2009 Citizens United Supreme Court decision.]

- *Do those who favor increased public monitoring of the operations of oil refineries, chemical manufacturers, paper mills, silicon chip makers, hospitals, or other plants generating toxic waste or emissions know that corporations can deny access to their premises by citizens wishing to determine whether government regulations are being followed?* **Personhood means that corporations are protected from warrantless search and seizure.**

- *Do supporters of local, independent businesses know that citizens cannot limit access by, or create special requirements for, any corporation that wishes to conduct business in their community?* **Corporate personhood means that such practices would infringe on corporate rights to equal protection.**

- *Do labor rights supporters know that people lose their rights to free speech and freedom of association, as well as other Bill of Rights protections, when on corporate property?* **Personhood reinforces a corporation's private property rights.**

Regulatory Agency Laws: Regulatory agencies are another method used by the U.S. elite to consolidate and increase their wealth and power. Most U.S. citizens believe that regulatory agencies were created to operate in the public's behalf to minimize harm done by corporations. This is not so.

One of the introductory questions in the Women's International League for Peace & Freedom (WILPF) study "Challenge Corporate Power: Assert the People's Rights" is this: *Don't regulatory agencies effectively monitor corporations and protect citizens and the environment from harm? The answer states that the reverse is true: Regulatory agencies are one of the biggest public relations success stories in the U.S. The first such agency, the* **Interstate Commerce Commission (ICC)**, *was created in 1887 to mollify a public sick of railroad corruption. But the ICC was actually a creation of the railroad executives. Weary from years of fierce price cutting and rate wars, and wary of populist uprisings against them, they hatched a plan to protect themselves from consumers and each other. The ICC was so successful for the railroads that other industries — such as insurance, meat packing, food, banking, and communications — soon acquired their own regulatory agencies.*

These big corporate players sought an escape from the rigors of competition through control of markets, government-borne costs of infrastructure and quality control, and direct or indirect price maintenance or guaranteed rates of return. But even though the government provides these services with taxpayer dollars, all profits still belong to the stockholders and owners. Criticism by those who saw through the charade began with the ICC and has resurfaced periodically, but regulatory agencies remain because they effectively protect the corporations that control politicians today as much as — or more than — they did at the end of the 19th century.

It is all too easy to find collusion between corporations and the agencies that are supposed to regulate them — not unlike the relationship between the Pentagon and military contracting corporations. Former officials with the Food and Drug Administration, for example, can be found in the executive ranks of companies like Monsanto, and vice versa. Corporations are allowed to submit their own research data providing product efficacy and safety, but since the data is classified as a trade secret, it's not available to the wider scientific community for verification. Academic institutions further complicate the mix. A revolving door between universities and agencies also exists, and corporations often provide significant funding for "independent" research that invariably supports the products and services under consideration.

LESSON 4: CORPORATIONS 57

Even when committed people work for them, regulatory agencies are underfunded, understaffed, and usurped by powerful legislators who are influenced by campaign contributions and constituent pressure for jobs. What's more, regulatory agencies make great red herrings. Corporate public relations teams blame them for economic ills and bureaucratic delays, and the public blames them for not doing their jobs. Attention is deflected away from corporations as the source of the problems and toward efforts to reform regulatory agencies. That the concept of the regulatory agency is inherently flawed doesn't even make it into the discussion. Until we can move this idea to the center of our debates, we cannot open up new strategies for change and greater democracy.

Property Rights Clauses of U.S. Constitution: While greatly revered, this document institutionalized the dominance of large commercial interests over small businessmen, artisans, and the general public. The U.S. elite use this Constitutional bias towards wealth to their own advantage. Peter Kelllman writing in "Rachel's Environment and Health Weekly #698" (May 25, 2000) explains this: *In 1776, the 13 colonies declared their independence from the British Crown and in 1781 the former colonies, now states, ratified a set of rules called the* **Articles of Confederation** *which determined their relationship to each other. In 1787 the state legislatures sent delegates to a meeting to discuss amending the Articles of Confederation. This meeting is now known as the* **Constitutional Convention of 1787***.*

Much had happened between 1781 and 1787 that caused the class of people who fomented the revolution to be concerned about their future. Divisions within the propertied class surfaced in the state legislatures and conflict between classes manifested itself in armed insurrections against the authority of state governments. In the state legislatures, the interests of the business owners and artisans clashed with those of the large commercial organizations. The small businessmen wanted high state tariffs to protect their small concerns, while those with large commercial interests demanded so-called "free trade" between the states. Meanwhile, the people who were clearing the land wanted to own it and armed insurrection against state authority broke out in many places. For example, the rebellion of Vermont's Green Mountain Boys against their New York landlords eventually led to the establishment of Vermont as the 14th state in 1777. But it was **Shay's Rebellion***, the armed insurrection of western Massachusetts farmers against the policies of the commercial class in Boston in 1786-1787, that weighed most heavily on the large property owners who sat down in 1787 to write the* **Constitution of the United States***. Those who wanted free trade between the states saw the need to have a strong federal government and federal army that would always be available to put down rebellions that could not be suppressed by state militias.*

The large commercial interests prevailed. Clauses in the Constitution that reflect the ascendancy of the large commercial interests over small business-owners are described by Kellman:

- **The Commerce Clause.** *The Commerce Clause of the Constitution, Article 1, Sec. 8(3), was created to straighten out the conflict of interest between the small and large property owners. After the Constitution was ratified independent state legislatures were no longer able to erect protective tariffs that "hindered" the flow of goods between the states. The big commercial interests of the day had triumphed over the small enterprises trying to "grow" local businesses.*

- **The Contracts Clause.** *Article I, Sec. 10. Legal theory holds that contracts are agreements made between equals, and therefore the state should not meddle... The founding fathers would have us believe that an indentured servant negotiating a contract with his master was somehow equal to the master at the negotiating table. The situation is similar to a small local union* *with 200 members negotiating a contract with a large employer who brings to the table enough resources to move the plant. In practice this can hardly be called a contract negotiated between equals. But this is the legal fiction, and the courts, congress, national guard, army, and police uphold this distortion of common sense.*

- **The Return Servants Clause.** *Article IV, Sec. 2(3) says: "No person held in Service of Labour in one State, under the laws thereof, escaping into another, shall, in consequence of any regulation therein, be discharged from such Service or labor, but shall be delivered up on Claim of the Party to whom such Service of labour may be due." Men like James Madison and George Washington wanted their human property, slaves and indentured servants, to know that if they escaped into another state the Constitution of the United States guaranteed their return.*

The concept of property rights over human rights has been enshrined in the Constitution even though property rights are very different from the other rights granted in the Constitution. Noam Chomsky, in an interview with David Barsamian (February, 1997) reminds us of the uniqueness of property rights: *Remember, contrary to what [James] Madison and a lot of modern political theorists tacitly assume, property rights are not like other rights. If I have the right of free speech, it doesn't interfere with your right of free speech. But if I have property, it interferes with your right to have that same property: you don't have it; I do. So the right to property is very different from the right to freedom of speech.*

MESSAGE IN SPEECH BALLOON OF FIGURE TRAMPLING ON PAPER THAT STATES: "CORPORATIONS SHOULD BE ALLOWED TO EXIST ONLY TO PROVIDE A PUBLIC SERVICE":

The original purpose of corporations "to provide a public service" has been thoroughly undermined by the U.S. elite. Through law and tradition the purpose has become "***to maximize profits to shareholders***". This change has had a very damaging effect on the democratic process in the U. S. as well as having devastating effects on the environment and the Global South poor.

Since corporations are the "property" of the shareholders and property rights are greater than human rights, society has not been wholly successful in making certain that corporate performance serves the public interest as well as the interests of owners and managers. Jim Hightower in his book *If the Gods Had Meant Us to Vote, They Would Have given Us Candidates* comments on this dilemma: *To the built-in irresponsibility of the amorphous corporate entity, add the bottom-line imperative of the CEO and board of directors. Academicians, judges, and corporate executives themselves aver that the sole role of corporate management is to make as much money as possible for the shareholders (a group that prominently includes the managers). The managers have no responsibility – none – to workers, environment, consumers, community, flag, or anything else. To the contrary, the entire incentive is for management to cut corners, to shortchange, to exploit. It is not a matter of a CEO's good intentions or bad – it is the bottom line, and it must be served. Put away all hope, ye who go in asking corporations to be "good", "responsible", "accountable". It is not in their self-interest or in their nature – you might as well expect a Rottweiler to meow.*

Corporations see no limit to what can, and therefore should be, privatized. The huge service sector (70% of the U.S. economy and more than 60% of the global economy) was up for grabs when the ***General Agreement on Trade in Services (GATS)*** was adopted in 1995 as part of the ***World Trade Organization (WTO)***. Vandana Shiva in a speech (March 26, 2001) had warned:

LESSON 4: CORPORATIONS

Every aspect of our lives is up for sale. Every aspect of human needs and every form of human activity is being redefined as a tradable service. A pamphlet "In Whose Service" published by Apex Press explains what the ramifications are: *Essential public services like health care, schools, and drinking water supply would be highly profitable to corporations if such services were fully privatized. Health care represents a $3.5 trillion market worldwide, while education is estimated to be worth $2 trillion dollars and water almost $1 trillion.*

Now international trade negotiations are taking place that promote the interests of corporations and investors. If adopted, these new rules will undercut the role of the public sector in providing essential social services to all regardless of income. The fundamental right to drinking water, public education, essential health care will be replaced by a profit-driven ideology that will undermine our democratic right to determine how essential services should be provided.

Robert Jensen in an article "Corporate Power is the Enemy of Our Democracy" published March 20, 2002 in the Long Island, NY Newsday asks this question: *Do Americans want to struggle to create a rich democracy, or are we going to roll over and accept a democracy for the rich?* After enumerating a long list of actions beneficial to corporations, Jensen poses another question: *Could there be a pattern here? Could it be that politicians, who are supposed to represent "we the people", sometimes pursue agendas that benefit only the few people and corporations with the resources to put (and keep) them in power? Could the obvious be true – that a country with an economy dominated by large corporations will find itself stuck with a politics dominated by those same corporations – and that ordinary people don't fare very well in such a system?*

When the Enron debacle broke, politicians eager to distance themselves from the mess argued it was a business scandal, not a political one. One lesson of Enron is that there is no distinction: A business scandal involving a large corporation is by definition a political scandal in a nation where corporations dominate the political sphere.

By law and tradition, corporations exist for one reason only: to maximize profit. Neither history nor logic gives any reason to think that profit-maximizing leads to meaningful democracy. Corporations are undemocratic internally and usually hostile to democracy externally. U.S. corporations do their best to subvert meaningful democracy at home through bribes to politicians, commonly called campaign contributions. They have shown repeatedly in other countries that they prefer dictatorships and oligarchies to real democracies; authoritarian governments are much easier to cut a deal with.

Although politicians and pundits are often very good at avoiding the obvious, it's hard not to notice that the concentration of economic power in the hands of a few has long had a corrosive effect on democracy.

Chris Hedges in an article entitled "Vast Underclass Must Rise Up Against Global Mafia or Die" (Truthout 5/20/13) concurs in the corrosive potential of corporations: *Corporations write our legislation. They control our systems of information. They manage the political theater of electoral politics and impose our educational curriculum. They have decimated labor unions and other independent mass organizations, as well as having bought off the Democratic Party, which once defended the rights of workers. With the evisceration of piecemeal and incremental reform – the primary role of liberal, democratic institutions – we are left defenseless against corporate power.*

Large corporations are in the process of gaining more and more power at the expense of democratic decision-making by "We the people". The next lesson explains the mechanisms used by large corporations and their supporting governments and other elite to maintain international control.

LESSON 5:
INTERNATIONAL CONTROL MECHANISMS
DISCUSSION QUESTIONS

1. What effect, if any, has the European conquest and colonization of less developed areas of the world had on the economic and political situation that exists today? For the nations of the Global North? For the nations of the Global South?

2. What are some of the differences between what you learned about U.S. and world history in a school setting and what is expressed in this lesson?

3. How do you think the elite justify the great disparity in wealth within countries and between countries?

4. Before reading this lesson, what did you assume was the main criteria for determining U.S. foreign aid to nations of the Global South?

5. What is your understanding of the World Trade Organization (WTO) and related agencies? Why do you think they are the object of citizen protests?

6. Is it fair to say that the priorities of the elite policy-makers are different than those of the majority of U.S. citizens?

7. What is the role of the Central Intelligence Agency (CIA) in maintaining a "stable business climate" worldwide?

OTHER POINTS OF DISCUSSION

The Syrian refugee crisis has been in the news lately. While there's certainly a conversation taking place about refugees—who they are, where they're going, who's helping them, and who isn't—what's absent is a discussion on how to prevent these wars from starting in the first place. Media outlets and political talking heads have found many opportunities to point fingers in the blame game, but not one media organization has accurately broken down what's driving the chaos: control over gas, oil and resources.

Indeed it's worth asking: How did demonstrations held by "hundreds" of protesters demanding economic change in Syria four years ago devolve into a deadly sectarian civil war, fanning the flames of extremism haunting the world today and creating the world's second largest refugee crisis? While the media points its finger to Syrian President Bashar Assad's barrel bombs and political analysts call for more airstrikes against ISIS and harsher sanctions against Syria, we're four years into the crisis and most people have no idea how this war even got started. While there is no question that the Syrian government is responsible for many of the casualties resulting from its brutal crackdown, this is not just a Syrian problem. Foreign meddling in Syria began several years before the Syrian revolt erupted. The U.S., France, Britain, Qatar, Saudi Arabia and Turkey created a pact in 2012 called "The Group of Friends of the Syrian People", a name that couldn't be further from the truth. Their agenda was to divide [Sunnis and Shiites] and conquer in order to wreak havoc across Syria in view of overthrowing Syrian President Bashar Assad.

But it's important to note the timing: This coalition and meddling in Syria came about immediately on the heels of discussions of an Iran-Iraq-Syria gas pipeline that was to be built between 2014 and 2016 from Iran's giant South Pars field through Iraq and Syria. With a possible extension to Lebanon, it would eventually reach Europe, the target export market. The map on the left shows where this *"Islamic Pipeline"* would be located. Note that the proposed *"Western Pipeline"* (map on the right) also runs through Syria. Since Assad favors the Islamic pipeline route, we're seeing what happens when a Mid-East strongman decides not to support something the U.S wants to get done. Regime change—from hostile to U.S.—friendly—is a preferred method to accomplish a desired goal that ensures U.S. international control.

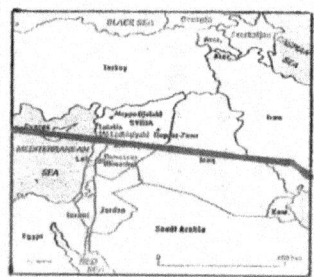 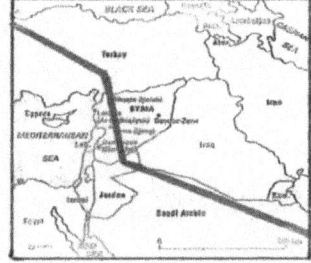

This essay is excerpted from an article by Mnar Muhawesh entitled "Migrant Crisis & Syrian War Fueled By Competing Gas Lines" (9/9/15).

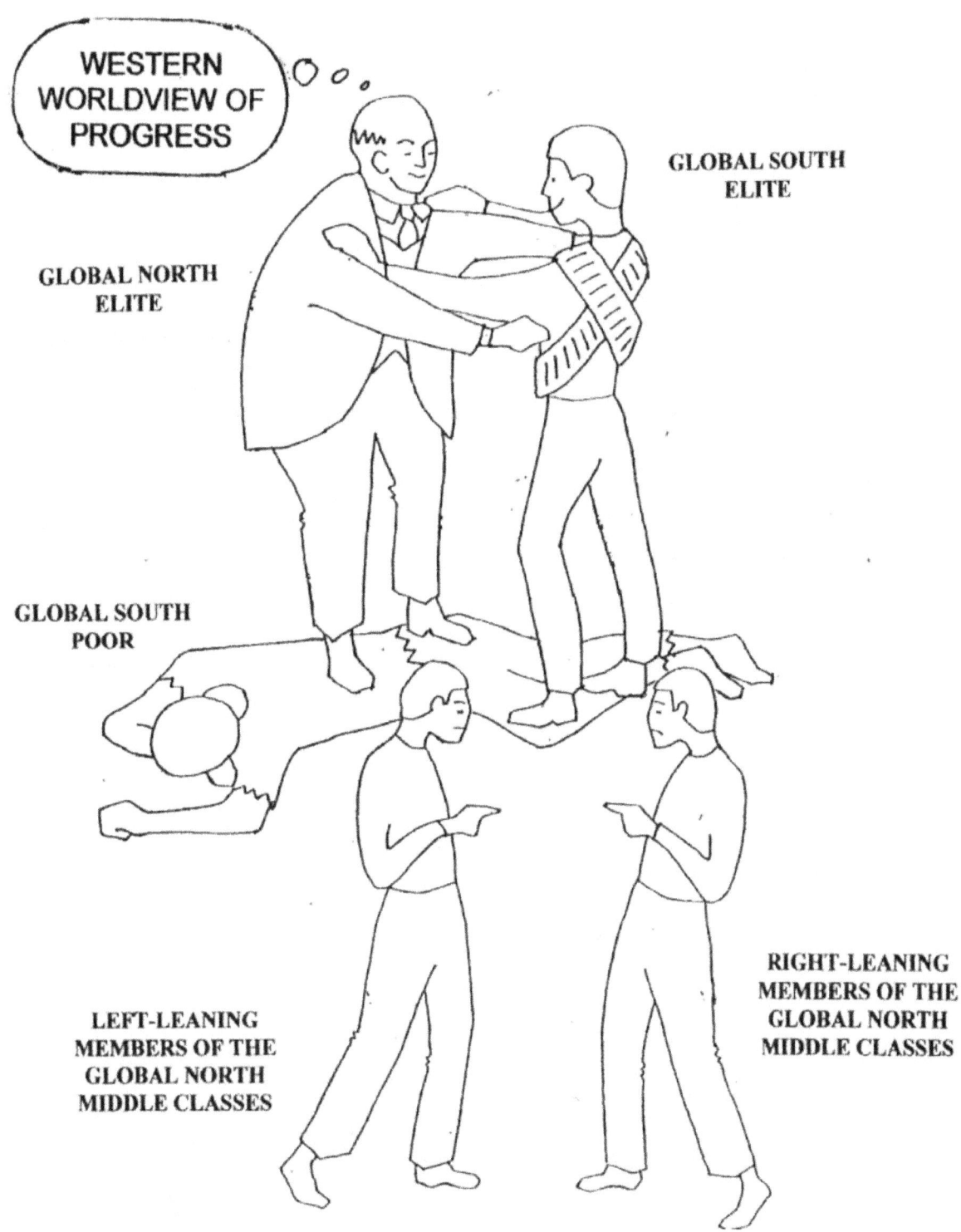

THE FOUR STANDING FIGURES:

The elite of the Global North and Global South and the supporting middle classes of the Global North. They represent 20% of the world's population and control in excess of 80% of the world's wealth with the top 1% controlling in excess of 40%.

FIGURE IN BUSINESS SUIT:

The elite of the Global North. Although Global North domination of the Global South has changed in *form* over the last 500 years, it has not changed in objective. That objective is and always has been: ***Global North control of the resources, labor, markets, and investment opportunities of the Global South in order that they can be used for the benefit of the Global North, especially the elite.***

FIGURE WEARING AMMUNITION BELT:

The "cooperative" ruling elite of the Global South. These governments are military or military-backed and are usually in alliance with the wealthy landowners and other elite sectors.

THE ELITE OF THE GLOBAL NORTH NATIONS AND THE COOPERATIVE ELITE OF THE GLOBAL SOUTH NATIONS EMBRACE:

The elite of the Global North nations financially and politically support the elite of the Global South nations who cooperate by creating/maintaining a favorable business climate for U.S. corporations.

THE TWO FIGURES IN THE FOREGROUND:

The Global North middle classes. In the U.S., the traditional liberal and conservative ideologies of the Democratic and Republican parties have largely morphed into a single pro-corporate ideology. The elite of *both* parties support the corporate agenda of economic globalization through U.S. imperialism. They encourage debate between the rank-and-file of the two parties who blame each other for national and international problems. The two factions appear unaware of the role they play in upholding the U.S. imperial system and the militarization and environmental damage that this entails. Third party attempts at opposition to the corporate agenda are effectively marginalized.

THE THOUGHT BALLOON:

The great majority of U.S. citizens share a common value system with the elite allowing for their acceptance of elite policy.

PRONE FIGURE:

The poor of the Global South. They represent 80% of the world's population and are either part of a poorly compensated labor force or, increasingly, are excluded from the economic globalization system altogether. Global North domination of the Global South has devastated the lives of the vast majority of the people of the Global South through the destruction of their traditional cultures and the decimation of their ancestral lands all done in the name of progress through economic development.

THE FOUR STANDING FIGURES:

The elite of the Global North and Global South and the supporting middle classes of the Global North. They represent 20% of the world's population and control in excess of 80% of the world's wealth with the top 1% controlling in excess of 40%.

FIGURE IN BUSINESS SUIT:

The elite of the Global North. Although Global North domination of the Global South has changed in form over the last 500 years, it has not changed its objective. That objective is and always has been: *Global North control of the resources, labor, markets, and investment opportunities of the Global South in order that they can be used for the benefit of the Global North, especially the elite.* How has the form changed? Initially, the Western European nations simply plundered the riches of the undeveloped areas of the world. Then they colonized the Global South to secure the same objectives. The colonial form of domination gave way in the twentieth century to a U.S.-led plan of economic globalization—a cooperative effort by the Global North nations—which, once again, would ensure that their desired objectives would be met.

The United States is the leading proponent of neoliberal economic policy, and before that, modern state capitalism. The U.S. has vigorously promoted them since the end of World War II when it acquired the position of economic leadership over the other Global North nations. How did the United States arrive at this position of unprecedented power? A brief history is in order. The United States was founded through revolution with the home-grown colonial elite gaining victory over their British counterparts. However, by adopting the language of the liberal *Enlightenment* thinkers to support their cause, the elite left the door wide open for the unintended result that the ordinary people would claim the same right of self-government for themselves that the elite had claimed in their *Declaration of Independence* from Great Britain. (The *U.S. Constitution*, adopted in 1789, granted the right to vote to approximately 10% of the population—the white male property-holding class.) U.S. history is largely a battle of the common people demanding the right of self-government for themselves, but with the elite holding fast to the conviction that they alone can rule the people in the best interest of all.

In the first half of the nineteenth century, powerful business interests in the North had determined that the economy of the young nation should be based on mechanical power (industrialization) rather than on human power (slavery). At this point the northern and southern states were developing very differently. The North was relying on immigrant labor for its industrial factories while the South was relying on slave labor for agricultural production. The North was seeking a protectionist foreign policy for its emerging industrial sector while the South, primarily an exporter of raw materials and importer of manufactured goods, preferred a "free trade" policy. These issues were settled only after a bitter civil war was fought with the northern industrialists emerging victorious. Once again, the *Civil War* was a battle of the elite classes—this time between the elite of the northern industrial states and the elite of the southern slave states. A northern victory and the preservation of the union not only assured the northern elite of an industrial-based economy and control of policy-making decisions, but also set the U.S. on its way to becoming the world's pre-eminent industrial power. The elite were challenged by, but withstood, a people's movement which came to be known as Populism in the closing decades of the 1800's.

A second theme of U.S. history is that of territorial expansion in order to accommodate the rapidly growing industrial sector and its need for resources and markets. *The Louisiana Purchase* (1803), the *War of 1812, the Mexican War* (1846-48) and the systematic removal of the indigenous population (ethnic cleansing) all served this purpose. In 1890, the Bureau of the Census officially declared that the interior U.S. frontier was closed. At that point, the elite debate was not if expansion should extend overseas, but simply *where* it should extend. The *Monroe Doctrine* (1823) had excluded European powers from the western hemisphere leaving control of the resources and markets of the newly independent Latin American nations solely to U.S. business interests. The *Spanish-American War* (1898), fought on the pretext of liberating Cuba from Spain, allowed access to a Pacific empire through the acquisition/annexation of Cuba, Puerto Rico, the Hawaiian Islands, Wake Island, Guam, and the Philippines. The U.S. elite preferred an *open door policy* (forcing open markets and access to resources) rather than direct colonial rule. This was a more sophisticated approach to imperialism, but no less effective.

While the U.S. elite (by now thoroughly capitalist) primarily faced internal struggles, the European capitalists, who now had virtual control of their national governments, primarily faced external struggles. They were forced to compete with each other for resources, disputed territory, and markets. One of the means they used to gain an advantage was by fanning the flames of nationalism to enlist the support of the common people. The tensions and conflicts between the European nations, as they all sought their own advantage, eventually erupted in the disastrous *First World War* (1914-1919).

Following World War I, a class struggle once again emerged in the United States. Farmers, workers, and small businessmen attacked big business for its connections with government, while accusing the government of being the servant of big business. The depression of the 1930's threatened the cozy relationship between big business and the government. There was a sharp increase in the number of *industrial unions* organized and they used strikes effectively, forcing the government to grant some concessions over the protests of big business. Turmoil existed in Europe as well. The unfair conditions placed on the defeated nations following World War I paved the way for the Fascist movement and the even more disastrous *Second World War* (1939-1945). Britain (along with the U.S.) had supported the corporate-friendly Fascist governments (Germany, Italy, Spain and others), seeing them as a bulwark against the spread of Communism which carried with it the threat of working class revolt as well as the fact that it offered an alternative economic system to that of capitalism.

World War II was a major turning point in international relations in two ways: First, with the advent of nuclear weapons, war between the industrialized nations was no longer feasible. Second, the United States emerged as the undisputed world economic leader.

The war helped, rather than hurt, the U.S. economy as it hastened the recovery from the depression while it devastated the other industrialized nations. By 1945, the U.S. controlled three-fourths of the world's invested capital and two-thirds of its industrial capacity. It enjoyed full employment and a flexible economy that easily adjusted to peacetime production. The United States was the world's most powerful and prosperous nation and many believed it was the destiny of the United States to extend its influence worldwide. How would this be accomplished? By instituting a system of economic globalization.

To facilitate the creation and maintenance of this system, which in its initial phase was termed *modern state capitalism*, the elite planners called for the founding of what became known as the *Bretton Woods institutions*. Convened by the United States and Great Britain, the United Nations Monetary and Financial Conference (held in July, 1944 at Bretton Woods, New Jersey) brought into being the institutions that would help ensure the success of modern state capitalism—the *International Monetary Fund (IMF)* and the *International Bank for Reconstruction and Development (the World Bank)*.

What would these financial institutions do? Since the planners' goal—a global capitalist economy—demanded economic growth, expanded world trade, and increased foreign direct investment, the IMF was designed to smooth world trade by reducing foreign exchange restrictions and by supplying a reserve fund for nations experiencing a temporary balance of payments problem. The World Bank was designed to make funds available for infrastructure projects and would promote private foreign investment. Decision-making power (who gets the loans and for what) in these institutions is vested in the donor nations and is proportional to the amount donated. Thus the leading donor, the United States, has the most decision-making power.

In order for this economic globalization plan to work, it was deemed necessary by U.S. policy-makers for U.S. corporations to maintain the advantage they had gained during World War II - the U.S. had escaped the widespread destruction of the war, while tripling its productive capacity because of it. The policy-makers came to the conclusion that it would be necessary to maintain a *"wartime economy"* indefinitely. Thus, the stage was set for the dominance of the *military-industrial complex* and for continuous warfare.

These post-war plans would require, at a minimum, free access to the raw materials of what was termed the *grand area* (the Western Hemisphere, the Far East, and the British Empire). This would be accomplished through economic and military domination of these parts of the world which the policy-makers correctly perceived the U.S. public would not support voluntarily. There was also the problem of domestic dissent. U.S. post-war policies were shaped with the recollection of the worker, farmer, and citizen movements of the 1930's in mind as well as the appeal that socialism and communism had held for the disenfranchised masses. The problem facing U.S. policy-makers was: how to control U.S. society without appearing to make alterations in its political and social forms. To this end they manufactured the *Communist threat* which proved successful in the attainment of these related goals—billions of dollars could be spent on Cold War armaments and the public could be scared into compliance with elite policy.

The second phase of economic globalization—neoliberalism—began in the early 1970's in response to the inability of nation-state governments to adequately meet the needs of corporations. It culminated in the establishment of the *World Trade Organization (WTO)* in 1995. The world was caught off guard in November/December 1999 when activists disrupted the WTO meetings held in Seattle, WA. What were they protesting? The anti-democratic nature of the WTO. Tony Clarke in a booklet "By What Authority!" describes the emergence of the WTO as a *global government*: From the outset, the World Trade Organization (WTO) was crafted like no other international agency. The architects of the final agenda for the Uruguay

Round wanted to put in place a political institution that would oversee the building of the new global economic order. In particular, the WTO would administer and enforce a body of rules governing the global economy which include the *General Agreement on Tariffs and Trade (GATT), Trade Related Investment Measures (TRIMS), Trade Related Intellectual Rights (TRIPS), General Agreement on Trade in Services (GATS),* to name a few. In order to undertake this mandate, the WTO needed to be equipped with the powers and tools of a global government. Over the past five years, the operations of the WTO show that it has acquired the judicial, legislative, and executive powers of *global governance.*

That the elite of the Global North had a long-term desire for, and actively worked toward, a world government under their control is made clear in the following quote from a speech delivered by **David Rockefeller** at the June 1991 Bilderberger meeting in which he thanks the media for their discretion in not exposing elite intentions in this regard: We are grateful to the Washington Post, the New York Times, Time Magazine *and other great publications whose directors have attended our meetings and respected their promises of discretion for almost forty years. It would have been impossible for us to develop our plan for the world if we had been subjected to the lights of publicity during those years. But, the world is more sophisticated and prepared to march towards a world government [emphasis added]. The supranational sovereignty of an intellectual elite and world bankers is surely preferable to the national autodetermination practiced in past centuries.*

FIGURE WEARING AMMUNITION BELT:

The "cooperative" ruling elite of the Global South. These governments are military or military-backed and are usually in alliance with the wealthy landowners and other elite sectors. These dictators/regimes have little regard for the basic human rights of the people they govern. Simply put, the "needs" of business are not compatible with the realization of basic human rights for the great majority of the people of the Global South. Political democracy is allowed and encouraged as long as the elected government remains "friendly" to the interests of U.S. business. *Economic democracy* (the right to adequate food, shelter, clothing, health care, and education) is never even a consideration.

THE ELITE OF THE GLOBAL NORTH NATIONS AND THE COOPERATIVE ELITE OF THE GLOBAL SOUTH NATIONS EMBRACE:

The elite of the Global North nations financially and politically support the elite of the Global South nations who cooperate by maintaining "stability" (subduing their own population, often by force) and creating/ maintaining a favorable business climate for U.S. corporations. A favorable business climate consists of easy access to cheap resources, a docile, inexpensive labor supply, unrestricted markets, and lucrative investment opportunities.

Steve Kangas in an essay "The Origins of the Overclass" describes the role played by the **Central Intelligence Agency (CIA)** in securing a "favorable business climate": *The CIA helps American corporations remain dominant in foreign markets by overthrowing governments hostile to unregulated capitalism and installing puppet regimes whose policies favor American corporations at the expense of their people.* This pattern of foreign policy was established early on by the Dulles brothers with **John Foster Dulles** serving as Secretary of State and **Allen Dulles** as the director of the CIA in the Eisenhower administration. The list of "friendly" governments (friendly to U.S. business, that is, not their citizens) supported by the U.S. included/includes some of the most ruthless regimes/tyrants imaginable: Italy (Mussolini), Germany (Hitler), Spain

LESSON 5: INTERNATIONAL CONTROL MECHANISMS

(Franco), South Africa, Iran (Shah of Iran), South Vietnam (Diem), Dominican Republic (Trujillo), Argentina, Uruguay, Brazil, Paraguay, Bolivia, Panama (Noriega), Nicaragua (Somoza), Cuba (Batista), Haiti (Duvalier), El Salvador, the Philippines (Marcos), Saudi Arabia, Zaire (Mobutu), Nigeria (Abacha), Indonesia (Suharto), Iraq (Hussein), Afghanistan (the Taliban) and Egypt (Mubarak).

Kangas in a related essay "A Timeline of CIA Atrocities" explains the downside of CIA intervention: *The ironic thing about all this intervention is that it frequently fails to achieve American objectives. Often the newly installed dictator grows comfortable with the security apparatus the CIA has built for him. He becomes an expert at running a police state. And because the dictator knows he cannot be overthrown, he becomes independent and defiant of Washington's will. The CIA then finds it cannot overthrow him, because the police and military are under the dictator's control, afraid to cooperate with American spies for fear of torture and execution. The only two options for the U.S. at this point are impotence or war.* Recent examples of this "boomerang" effect are General Noriega (Panama), Saddam Hussein (Iraq), and the Taliban government of Afghanistan, all three brought to power by the CIA.

At first, the "subduing of the population" of the Global South nations was effected by direct U.S. military action as in Korea (technically a UN intervention) and Vietnam, but the unsuccessful Vietnam experience necessitated a change in tactics (but not objectives). **Low Intensity Conflict (LIC)** was introduced to placate the U.S. public while still keeping the relationships with the Global South governments in place. Local military and paramilitary units are financed and trained by the U.S. to eliminate the necessity of sending in U.S. troops. Increasingly, however, the elite planners realized that control of Global South populations could best be effected primarily through economic means. This eliminates the negative image projected by repressive dictators/regimes. The IMF and World Bank use their ability to grant or refuse loans as leverage on Global South governments to ensure that they comply with the goals of the Global North elite.

The governments of those nations who choose not to "cooperate", but rather, attempt to use their resources for the benefit of their own people, are severely penalized. The U.S., through the CIA and, since the early 1980's, the *National Endowment for Democracy (NED)*, has found it necessary to "destabilize" (destroy) these "unfriendly" governments. Examples are: Iran (1953); Guatemala (1954); The Congo (1960); Brazil (1964); the Dominican Republican and Indonesia (1965); Bolivia (1970-71); Chile (1973), Haiti (1991 and 2004); Honduras (2009). An unsuccessful attempt was made in Cuba (1961).

Why is it necessary for the U.S. to destroy these governments since most of them represent small, poor, unimportant countries? According to the **Virus of Independent Development Theory** (also known as the **Domino Theory**), a small independent nation that could serve as an example to other small nations looms as a threat to the economic globalization plan and must be avoided at all costs.

As the elite planners expected, conflict is no longer between industrialized nation-states who covet the same resources or territory as in the major world wars. Rather, it is between Western capital with its perceived "right" to the resources of the world (since they can most efficiently develop them) and the ordinary people of the Global South. These conflicts are often "civil wars" with government forces or mercenary soldiers battling their own people who are opposed to the often harsh and discriminatory government policies which primarily benefit the elite and foreign investors and corporations.

The corporations gain in two ways: their access to resources, labor, markets, and investment opportunities is preserved and those financial institutions that grant loans for weapon purchases and those corporations that manufacture the weapons (over half of total sales are made by U.S. corporations) have a ready market for their loans and products, often supplying both sides in a given conflict. Increasingly, the U.S. government is privatizing services formerly performed by the military (such as food service and the building of bases), as well as awarding no-bid contracts to favored corporations for the reconstruction of the damage caused by the military. Corporations benefit greatly from war and its aftermath while the poor of the world suffer.

THE TWO FIGURES IN THE FOREGROUND:

The Global North middle classes. In the U.S., the traditional liberal and conservative ideologies of the Democratic and Republican parties have largely morphed into a single pro-corporate ideology. The elite of both parties support the corporate agenda of economic globalization through U.S. imperialism. They encourage debate between the rank-and-file of the two parties who blame each other for national and international problems. The two factions appear unaware of the role they play in upholding the U.S. imperial system and the militarization and environmental damage that this entails. Third party attempts at opposition to the corporate agenda are effectively marginalized.

While many U.S. citizens recognize the negative impacts of environmental degradation, the looming climate change crisis, and the wars in Afghanistan and Iraq, they do not connect these issues to the U.S. foreign policy of demanding access to Global South resources. The 2003 U.S. invasion of Iraq is an obvious example of this connection. The *Carter Doctrine* of January 23, 1980 designated the secure flow of Persian Gulf oil as a "vital interest of the United States". Michael Klare in his book *Blood and Oil: The Dangers and Consequences of America's Growing Dependency on Imported Petroleum* states: *Claiming that this key interest* [the secure flow of Persian Gulf oil] *was threatened by the Soviet occupation of Afghanistan (which had begun in December 1979) and the near-simultaneous rise of a radical Islamic regime in Iran, President Jimmy Carter told Congress that Washington would use "any means necessary, including military force" to keep the oil flowing.* **The Central Control (Centcom)** was established on January 1, 1983 to implement the Carter Doctrine. Thus, the Iraq War and occupation is merely the latest application of a long-standing policy supported by all the administrations from Carter to Trump. The Carter Doctrine was foreshadowed by the agreement between President Roosevelt and Ibn Saud of Saudi Arabia which promised U.S. protection of the Saudi royal family in exchange for the flow of oil to the U.S.

THE THOUGHT BALLOON:

The great majority of U.S. citizens share a common value system with the elite allowing for their acceptance of elite policy. Admittedly, the elite go to great lengths to confuse and mislead the public by using the rhetoric of "spreading freedom and democracy throughout the world" while advancing their agenda of economic globalization. In doing this, they have the cooperation of the corporate-owned mass media and, usually, the cooperation of the religious and educational systems. The promulgation and internalization of the Western world view of progress has allowed colonialism, the near annihilation of the Native American population, the enslaving of Africans, and today, allows the continuing oppression of the Global South poor.

THE PRONE FIGURE:

The poor of the Global South. They represent 80% of the world's population and are either part of a poorly compensated labor force or, increasingly, are excluded from the economic globalization system altogether. Global North domination of the Global South has devastated the lives of the vast majority of the people of the Global South through the destruction of their traditional cultures and the decimation of their ancestral lands which is all done in the name of progress through economic development.

When direct colonial rule became too costly (socially and financially), the elite retained their dominance of the nations of the Global South through economic means—"development" programs, primarily export agriculture, and then, off-shore manufacturing. The purpose of the colonial system had been to supply resources and markets for the "mother" country. The colonizers destroyed the existing native economies (often barter systems) and their social and political structures in order to implement a system of cash crops for export and extraction of raw materials. The majority of the people were forced off the land and cash crops for export replaced food crops for the people. The people, uprooted from their land and communities, simply did not have the wherewithal to compete in the "money" economy. Global South nations under IMF/World Bank tutelage have seen infant mortality rates increase, schools and housing deteriorate, unemployment skyrocket, and the general health of the people decline. Statistics show: there are more poor people today than ever before; there is an accelerating gap between the rich and the poor; widespread violence is tearing families and communities apart nearly everywhere; and the planet's ecosystems are deteriorating at an alarming rate.

Why is this happening? As the Global North elite vigorously pursue their goal of economic globalization, they continue to make two crucial errors. First, they assume that it will benefit everyone. It does not. As the international financial institutions and the transnational corporations and their major investors see their profits increase, the labor forces of poor countries are forced to compete against each other in a "race to the bottom". Wealth has not "trickled down" to the poor; rather, the reverse has occurred. Second, they assume there are no limits to economic growth. The earth which supplies the raw materials does have a finite supply of resources, as well as a limited ability to absorb the massive amount of waste produced by the industrial process.

The World Bank did make attempts in the 1970's to address poverty in the Global South. It was assumed that "backward" societies must be modernized through economic growth and industrialization. This provided a boon for those in the Global North nations who provided the capital and inputs for the "development" projects. These efforts benefited some in the Global South (usually the already well-to-do), but those without land or resources (the majority) did not benefit and the loans made for these projects would come back to haunt these countries.

If the 1970's was a decade of well-intentioned, but ill-advised, projects promoted by the World Bank, the 1980's was a totally different story. The 1960's and 1970's had been marked by the growth of a more assertive and unified Global South. The success of the OPEC nations in 1973 to seize control of the price of oil spurred other Global South nations to attempt to create cartels in other commodities. Although these attempts failed, it gave the elite of the Global North a bad scare. This Global South economic challenge coincided with two other direct (and humiliating) threats to U.S. hegemony: their military defeat in Vietnam (1975) and the Iran hostage crisis (1979-1981).

The Reagan administration came to power in 1981 with an agenda to discipline the Global South. While U.S. military adventures against radical Global South movements dominated the news, perhaps more lethal was the economic warfare the U.S. unleashed against the Global South on a global scale. The U.S.-dominated World Bank spear- headed the effort. In the 1980's, as interest rates rose to unprecedented heights, it became difficult for the Global South to service the huge loans made to them in the 1970's. The World Bank and IMF (with the same agenda) made the acceptance of **Structural Adjustment Programs** (SAP's) a condition for the rescheduling of Global South debt.

Ostensibly promoted for "efficiency", the primary purpose of the SAP's was to undercut the attempt by the Global South nations to gain greater economic independence at the national level and income redistribution at the global level. They are also designed to facilitate repayment of debt owed to wealthy investors and bankers in the Global North, but are, first and foremost, a means of controlling the economies of Global South nations to the benefit of the Global North. Economic domination has become the Global North's tool of choice in exercising international control of the Global South.

The next lesson explains how the elite exercise domestic control through the U.S. class system in a supposedly classless society.

LESSON 6:
DOMESTIC CONTROL MECHANISMS
DISCUSSION QUESTIONS

1. Which of the four classes described in this lesson do you feel a part of? Or do you feel that there are no classes in U.S. society?

2. How is dissent of elite policy discouraged through the U.S. class system?

3. Do you feel any sense of control by the social class/classes above you? In what way?

4. Do you feel any sense of control over the social class/classes below you? In what way?

5. The role of the professional-managerial class in U.S. society is critical. How are members of that class rewarded for supporting elite policy? How are they disciplined if they do not?

6. Was the War on Poverty in the 1960's a realistic goal? Why is there so much poverty in the world's richest country?

7. What role, if any, does the underclass play in U.S. society?

OTHER POINTS OF DISCUSSION

Why does the U.S. public accept the inequitable world order described in the previous lesson? And why do they accept the inequities built into U.S. society? Both of these result from the fact that a very small group of people control vast amounts of wealth and power—a fact that is hidden from U.S. citizens in various ways. We receive most of our information through the mass media, but possibly our more enduring "lessons" are learned from "authority figures".

The most influential of these are, for many people, teachers and clergy who are members of what I have termed the professional-managerial class. These people are the "opinion makers" of the country. They are the people we trust and depend on to give us unbiased information. Why don't these "experts" give us a more accurate picture of reality? Philip Berrigan, a former Roman Catholic priest, describes the effects of his seminary education in these words from his autobiography, *Fighting the Lamb's War:*

Priests were mass-produced to be silent, to be conformists, and to be patrons of the government. Like most of our counterparts in colleges, universities, public schools and seminaries, we were taught to believe in the capitalist system, never questioning how a system that poisons the environment, imprisons and executes the poor, and thrives on war, could be compatible with the teachings of Christ.

It should come as no surprise, that if this is the training men receive when they enter the Roman Catholic priesthood, that Berrigan's assessment of the church would be as follows:

We operate as though, under a divine and magical star, we will muddle through with minimal losses while grace and providence work for us—providing, however, we pretend hard enough that nuclear overkill does not exist, that genocide in Indochina has not been carried out, that the North Atlantic community does not control one-half of the world's wealth, that wealth and power are not identified with the white world, and poverty and desperation are not identified with the so-called colored world. The church in America—in fact, in the West as a whole—has accepted as religion a kind of cultural syncretism, culminating in near-perfect allegiance to the State.

Furthermore, no Bishop has questioned the marriage of Big Business and Big Military in Big Government, and how the marriage results in government by and for the wealthy and powerful. No Bishop has condemned the American rape of the developing world, nor the arms race in horror weapons, nor American arms salesmanship, nor the division of the world by superpowers.

The educational system is no different. Many thoughtful and caring people enter this profession. It makes the control of the population all the more insidious when these people aren't even conscious of the fact that they are deceiving the very people they have pledged to serve to the benefit of the ruling elite.

LESSON 6: DOMESTIC CONTROL MECHANISMS

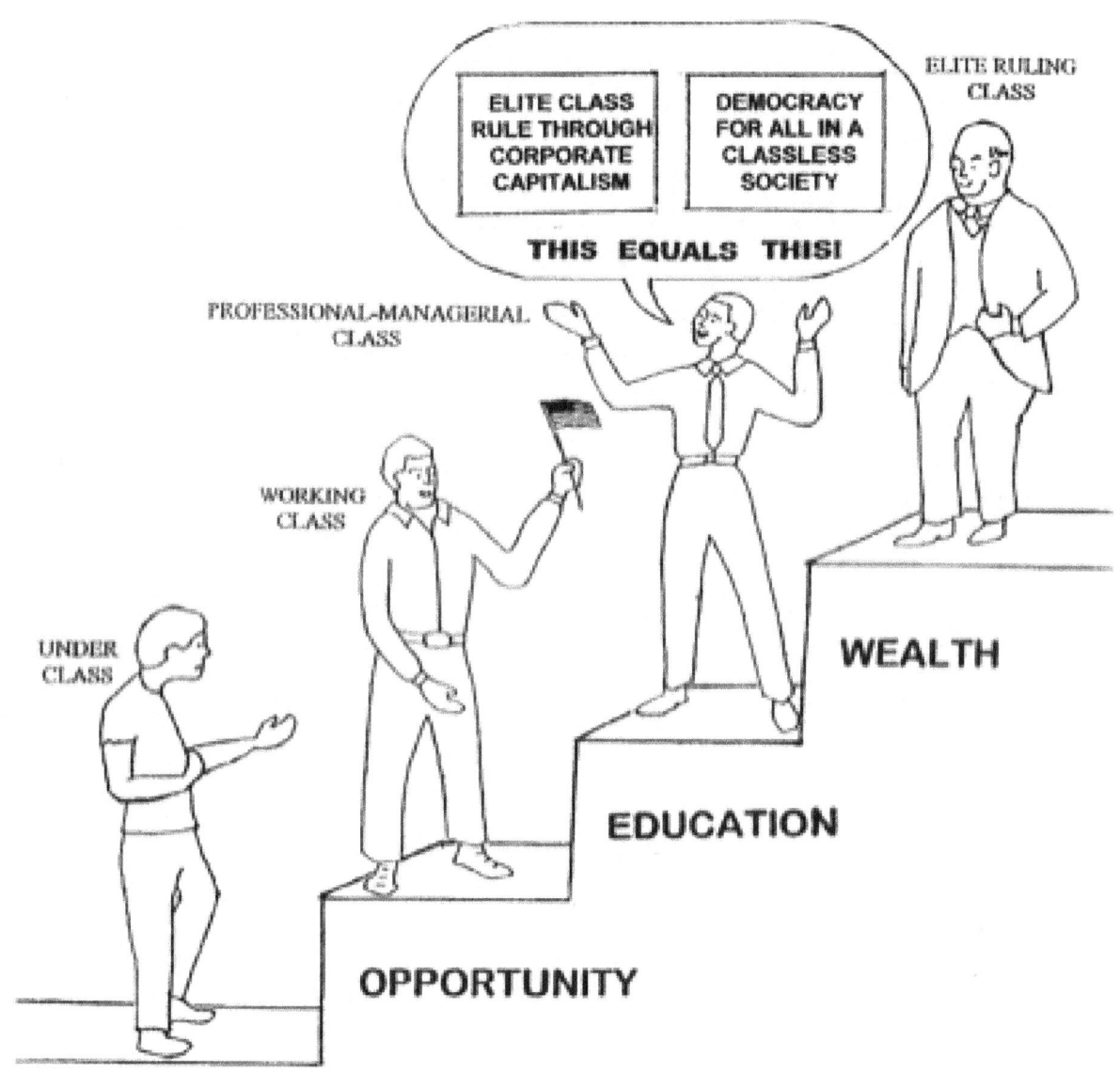

FIGURE ON TOP STEP:

The elite ruling class. They are largely invisible in U.S. society since the professional-managerial class acts as a buffer between it and the working and underclasses.

FIGURE ON THIRD STEP:

The professional-managerial class. They are roughly the 20 percent of the population who are educated, articulate, and are expected to play some role in decision making. Their positions and prestige are dependent upon their willingness to support the economic and social policies of the elite ruling class, consciously or, even better, unconsciously.

They are the people whose economic and social status is based on education and expertise rather than on ownership of capital or property. This is what distinguishes them from the elite ruling class—they must work for a living while the elite do not. Yet, in relation to the working and under classes, they are an elite based on their income, authority, influence, and power. This class includes college and university teachers, clergy, journalists, political pundits, business and military leaders and other "experts".

MESSAGE IN SPEECH BALLOON:

Essentially, the professional-managerial class function as social managers. They "interpret" the elite ruling class's policies to the people through many different avenues including simply not taking a position against them. Foreign policy, which is dependent upon the oppression of the majority of people of the Global South in the interest of the business and investor class (elite ruling class), is interpreted as the advance of peace and democracy worldwide. Domestic policy, which assures that the elite ruling class is subsidized by the labor of the working and underclass, is interpreted as upholding the values of a classless society.

FIGURE ON THE SECOND STEP:

The working class. For the most part they willingly and patriotically support the government.

FIGURE ON BOTTOM STEP:

The underclass (disadvantaged working class). This class is made up largely of people of color. They are born into this class and have little opportunity to rise to a higher level. THE

STEPS:

They represent the barriers between the classes. The extreme wealth of the elite ruling class is the barrier between it and the professional-managerial class. The extensive education and training of the professional-managerial class is the barrier between it and the working class. Increased opportunity, usually related to race, is the barrier between the working class and the underclass. Each class has control over the class/classes below it to a greater or lesser degree which helps to perpetuate the class system in the United States.

The elite ruling class. They are largely invisible in U.S. society since the professional-managerial class acts as a buffer between it and the working and under classes. Note: Much of the material in the next three sections is based on ideas expressed in Barbara Ehrenreich's book *Fear of Falling*. However, for the group of people who she describes as the "middle class" I have chosen to use the term "professional-managerial class".

FIGURE ON THIRD STEP:

The professional-managerial class. They are roughly the 20 percent of the population who are educated, articulate, and are expected to play some role in decision-making. Their positions and prestige are dependent upon their willingness to support the economic and social policies of the elite ruling class, consciously or, even better, unconsciously.

They are the people whose economic and social status is based on education and expertise rather than on ownership of capital or property. This is what distinguishes them from the elite ruling class—they must work for a living while the elite do not. Yet, in relation to the working and underclasses, they are an elite based on their income, authority, influence, and power. This class includes college and university teachers, clergy, journalists, political pundits, business and military leaders and other "experts".

The professions, as we know them today, arose between 1870 and 1920. The people who established them were the descendants of an older gentry of independent farmers, small businessmen, self-employed lawyers, doctors, and ministers who were being "squeezed out" by the powerful new capitalist class. Professionalism was, above all, a way to restrict entry into these occupations. The professionals erected educational and training barriers to prevent the classes below from entering. They succeeded in carving out an occupational monopoly restricted to the elite minority who could afford college educations and graduate degrees (about 5% of the population at that time).

The professions of management and engineering grew out of the early twentieth-century struggle between labor and capital. Up until this time, skilled craftsmen dominated both the technology and organization of the work process. It was determined by the capitalists that if the "mental" and "physical" work could be separated, capital could gain greater control over the workplace. The physical labor could be reduced to many simple, repetitive tasks performed by unskilled workers while the creative and organizational work could be performed by more reliable (in the eyes of the capitalists) professional managers and engineers. The way was paved for Henry Ford's assembly line and the labor unrest of the 1930's.

MESSAGE IN SPEECH BALLOON:

Essentially, the professional-managerial class functions as social managers. They "interpret" the elite ruling class's policies to the people through many different avenues including simply not taking a position against them. Foreign policy, which is dependent upon the oppression of the majority of people of the Global South in the interest of the business and investor class (elite ruling class), is interpreted as "the advance of peace and democracy worldwide". Domestic policy, which assures that the elite ruling class is subsidized by the labor of the working and under classes, is interpreted as "upholding the values of a classless society". The period in which the professions took shape (1870-1920) was a period of violent clashes between the working class and the capitalist class. Throughout this period, the knee-jerk capitalist response was repression—armed guards to break strikes and beatings, jailings, and lynchings to crush the militant leadership of the working class. The emerging professional-managerial class stepped into the fray in the role of peacemakers. Their message to the capitalists was that nonviolent social control would in the long run be more effective than brute force. Mines and mills did not have to be hotbeds of working-class sedition; they could be run more smoothly by trained, "scientific" managers. Working-class families did not have to be perpetual antagonists to capitalist society; they could be "Americanized" by teachers and social workers and eventually be won over to the new "consumer" lifestyle actively being promoted by business admen and marketing experts. Almost every profession, from sociology to home economics, had something to offer in the great task of "taming" the U.S. working class. In every field, professionalism was presented as a major reform in the interests of science, rationality, and public service. They believed all social problems could be transformed into technical problems which could only be solved by expanding the new class of professional experts. In this it was difficult to conceal their own class interests as they advocated the need for more and more "experts". This of course cost money, but the capitalist class opted in favor of the professional-managerial class to control society rather than an army of security guards. The professional-managerial class would act as a buffer between capital and labor. Labor's animosity could be directed at "management" rather than at the capitalist owners.

FIGURE ON SECOND STEP:

The working class. For the most part the working class willingly and patriotically supports the government. Although the 1920's and 1930's were a time of labor unrest and anti-capitalist feeling, this was reversed, somewhat, by the New Deal programs of the Roosevelt administration, and, ultimately, by the great industrial surge engendered by World War II.

In the wave of economic prosperity that followed the war, it looked as though the United States was moving toward the ideal of a classless society. The prosperity created by the war was shared broadly during the 1940's, 1950's, and into the 1960's. Although there was poverty within the U.S., prosperity was remarkably widespread. Many poor people were able to move up into the growing middle class and average citizens were affluent by practically any historical standard. It appeared to be a win-win situation—capitalists producing at record rates and the general population consuming at record rates.

The *consumer culture* had been born in the U.S. in the 1920's. Alan Durning in his book *How Much is Enough?* explains: *Economists and business executives, concerned that the output of mass production might go unsold when people's natural desires for food clothing, and shelter were satisfied, began pushing mass consumption as the key to economic expansion.*

Turning the frugal, self-reliant families of the U.S. into consumers was not an easy task, but one that succeeded beyond even the most optimistic adman and business executive's expectations. The advertising industry and marketing experts created "wants" where none had previously existed and then turned "wants" into "needs". Consumption slowed during the depression and World War II, but came of age in the post-war economic boom. Western Europe, Japan and people with the means to do so throughout the world followed the U.S. example of a consumer life-style. Durning evaluates the impact that consumerism is having on human society and the environment:

LESSON 6: DOMESTIC CONTROL MECHANISMS

The wildfire spread of the consumer life-style around the world marks the most rapid and fundamental change in day-to-day existence the human species has ever experienced. Over a few short generations, we have become car drivers, television watchers, mall shoppers, and throwaway buyers. The tragic irony of this momentous transition is that the historic rise of the consumer society has been quite effective in harming the environment, but not in providing people with a fulfilling life.

However, mass consumption *appeared* to be benefiting everybody—business and the consumer—so that by the 1960's it was believed that all U.S. citizens could be brought into the economic mainstream. To do so the **War on Poverty** was declared by the Johnson administration in 1964. Scarcely twenty years later, in the 1980's war was declared, not on poverty, but on the poor themselves in the guise of welfare "reform". What had happened in the meantime?

The 1960's are remembered as a time of change. Nearly every U.S. institution was challenged, weighed in the balance, and found wanting—marriage, the nuclear family, religion, government, education, civil rights (or rather, the lack of them) based on race, sex, and creed, and the involvement in the Vietnam War.

Although the young were in the forefront of the movement, the mood of the nation supported change. Liberal reform appeared in almost every area of U.S. life. The civil rights movement gained a respected leader in **Dr. Martin Luther King, Jr.** and the support of the nation in general when abuses were exposed largely through the medium of television. Protest against the Vietnam War opened the nation's eyes, not only to the horror of modern warfare (again via television), but also to the question of whether or not the United States even had a right to interfere in the destinies of other nations. Welfare reform was enacted and gained a certain respectability. Abuses of business and industry were exposed. **Ralph Nader** led the fight for consumers' rights and a concern for the environment developed. People stood up and demanded to be heard.

The ruling elite's reaction to all of this was to declare a *"crisis in democracy"*—there was too much of it. In their eyes, "democracy" simply cannot withstand this type of an assault on the established order of things. The problem was: how to return the public to their usual apathetic condition. The Liberal bipartisan consensus (that had developed in response to the disruption caused by the depression) was seen as the cause of the turmoil. It would have to be eliminated.

In the political arena, the **debt crisis** was manufactured to reverse the trend of citizen democracy so feared by the elite. According to David Stockman, the first Director of the Office of Management and Budget of the Reagan administration, the large-scale strategic goal of the Reagan planners was: to cap social spending by increasing government debt. Increasing government debt was accomplished through (1) huge increases in military spending, (2) tax reductions to the wealthy and to major corporations, and (3) the monetarist policy of high interest rates which compounded rising government deficits to unpayable levels. These deficits could then be used as the excuse to refuse further citizen demands and to eliminate existing social programs as well.

The Liberal elite, unwittingly, did their part. In the 1960's the Liberal experts advocated government programs to integrate the poor into mainstream society (that is, integrate the poor into working class society, not professional society). These programs were administered in a top-down manner that treated the poor in an often undignified and childlike way. Most of these programs (such as affirmative action and school bussing) were unpopular with the working class and with the poor themselves. In addition, the cost of the Vietnam War was becoming prohibitive. The U.S. could no longer afford both "guns" and "butter" so they opted for guns.

Then, to add insult to injury, the student unrest on college campuses across the nation targeted the core beliefs of the professional class: their authority as experts simply because of their education and training. Their programs in shambles, and their authority questioned by the very people who were expected to follow in their footsteps, the Liberals simply gave up in frustration and confusion.

This left the door wide open for a sharp turn towards *Conservatism* and a bipartisan Conservative consensus was engineered. The *New Right* was born in 1974. Wealthy Conservative businessmen funded numerous think tanks to further this effort. High on the New Right agenda was a pro-business plank - the need to shrink government in order to ensure truly "free" enterprise. It also projected itself as pro-family, pro-law-and-order, and anti-gun-control while it declared that immigrant rights and cultural diversity loomed as threats to these values. It adopted the Goldwater themes of militarism and anti-Communism and the Wallace themes of opposition to school busing, "liberal" textbooks, the Equal Rights Amendment, abortion, gay rights, the teaching of evolution and sex education while advocating prayer in school.

The New Right championed traditional values—hard work, self-denial, and family loyalty. However, no one seemed to notice that the New Right agenda was at odds with the consumer culture and capitalist activity, in general. In the 1950's the consumer culture had focused on products appropriate to suburban family living. In the late 1950's, however, it had identified youth as a distinct market who should spend "just for fun". Advertisements and products appealed to self-centeredness, impulsiveness, and the pursuit of personal pleasure, hardly traditional values.

Many young professionals were lured into the service of business and finance rather than to government programs. But with that change, the motivation of many in the professional class changed from public service (which was one of the original purposes of professionalism) to simply making money—lots of it. Greed became socially acceptable.

But the New Right couldn't blame "permissiveness" and the decline of traditional values on capitalism or consumerism. So who/what were to blame? The New Right declared that the villains were the Liberal elite and their support of government programs to aid the poor and their efforts to protect the rights of all citizens. The biggest culprit was welfare. Welfare created dependency and encouraged permissiveness since there was no need to form stable families, to work for a living, or to honor America's traditional values. They also targeted the Liberal elite's support of gay rights, women's right-to-choice, immigrant rights, and their tolerance of, indeed, their embracing of, cultural diversity.

In actuality, the blue/pink-collar working class was a burden and a natural antagonist to business interests. The populist language of the New Right conflicted openly with its aristocratic allegiances. While the New Right extolled the virtues of the working class, the government abetted the worst capitalist assault on working people since the 1920's—wages were cut, manufacturing jobs were out-sourced, capital was shifted from manufacturing to the quick-profit realm of financial speculation resulting in the "deindustrialization" of the United States. The members of the professional-managerial class who assisted this transformation relinquished the traits that had traditionally been attached to the professions—objectivity, scientific rationality, and a dispassionate concern for society—for the opportunity to get rich quick.

The *Moral Majority* was formed in 1979 to rally the disenchanted working class to the New Right agenda. The New Right succeeded in forging the improbable alliance of the business and the working class (both producers) against the poor and the Liberal elite (both non-producers). It exploited the alienation of powerless working class citizens to build a populist political base in support of an elitist pro-business/anti-labor agenda. In a quid pro quo—political access for political support—the conservative political/business elite agreed to politically advance the agenda of the religious right leadership in exchange for their political support and the political support of their followers. Many of these often well-intentioned, caring people, concerned about what they perceived to be a breakdown in public morality, became politically active for the first time believing that their efforts would help fulfill what they believed was the United States' rightful destiny—that of being a Christian nation.

But for many of these people, a Christian nation meant a white Christian nation. Already alarmed by the demographic trend towards an eventual non-white U.S. majority, the election of *Barack Obama* in 2008 as the first black U.S. president was an affront to these conservative Christians, as well as to many others. A further stressor was the economic wreckage caused by the 2008-2009 Wall Street collapse and the ensuing recession which adversely affected many people who had previously benefitted from the institutionalized privilege of white people. The myth of *individualism*—people get what they deserve (for ill or gain)—had allowed them to attribute their success to their own hard work and ingenuity and to blame the less fortunate for their unhappy plight, as well. But as their economic and social conditions deteriorated, this was no longer possible. What had gone wrong and who was to blame? Out of this discontent the *Tea (Taxed Enough Already) Party movement* was born. The Tea Party's call for fiscal responsibility, constitutionally limited government, free market economics, and a strong national defense dove-tail nicely with the corporate agenda of government deregulation, lower taxes, and a decrease in social spending. From behind the scenes the Tea Party is nurtured by conservative think tanks such as the Cato Institute and by conservative businessmen such as billionaire brothers, Charles and David Koch, who liberally finance the movement. Conservative media such as Fox News, owned by Rupert Murdoch, publicize it.

By co-opting this "grass roots" movement, corporate America is advancing its own agenda at the expense of those it pretends to support. The end result is that U.S. families, white and non-white alike, are being frayed and torn under the weight of too much work, too little time, too little income, and too few government supports. This process can be seen as a mechanism of domestic control. People simply do not have the time or energy to participate in community affairs let alone to concern themselves with the plight of people of the Global South whose land and resources are being plundered by giant corporations in the name of progress.

Adding to this deliberate assault on the working class was the decline of the *trade union movement*. This decline was directly related to the role technology was playing/would play in the displacement of workers. Jeremy Rifkin in his book *The End of Work* explains how this happened. Management simply declared that it wasn't a problem: *After years of growing concern over technology displacement, the long overdue debate on automation fizzled in the mid-1960's. Charles Silberman, writing in Fortune, declared that "the effects of automation on employment have been wildly and irresponsibly exaggerated."*

Rifkin, however, places some of the blame on organized labor: *The failure to adequately address the question of technological unemployment is partially the fault of organized labor. The voice of millions of working Americans, the labor movement waffled repeatedly on the issue of automation, only to eventually cast its lot with management, to the detriment of its own constituency.*

Having accepted both the inevitability and even desirability of laborsaving technology, labor began to lose the momentum it had enjoyed since the end of World War II. Boxed into a corner, the unions made a hasty retreat, shifting their collective bargaining demands from the issue of control over production and work processes to the call for job retraining. Employers were more than willing to concede to labor's new demands. The costs of introducing retraining programs was far less onerous that the prospect of a long and protracted battle with labor over the introduction of new, automated technologies on the shop floor.

By abandoning the question of control over the technology in favor of calls for retraining, the unions lost much of their effective bargaining power. Had control issues remained a strong priority, labor might have successfully negotiated collective bargaining agreements with management that would have ensured labor participation in productivity gains brought on by automation. Shorter workweeks and increased wages could have been tied to increases in productivity. Instead labor capitulated, contenting itself with defensive agreements that provided job security for older workers, phased attrition of the existing workforce, and limited retraining opportunities for its members as ways of dealing with automation.

In the end, the technological forces sweeping through the economy proved too powerful a foe. Their ranks thinned by wave after wave of new technological innovation, as well as by losses suffered at the hands of foreign competition, the nation's blue collar unions began their historic retreat and now exist as little more than a hollow reminder of their once pre-eminent role in American economic life.

FIGURE ON BOTTOM STEP:

The underclass (disadvantaged working class). It is composed largely of people of color. They are born into this class and have little opportunity to rise to a higher level. The income gap that at one point in time looked like it was bridgeable has become greater. In 1980, the incomes of the richest 1% of U.S. families equaled the income of families in the bottom 20%. A decade later, inequality doubled. That is, by 1990 the income of the top 1% was greater than the bottom 40%. Income inequality in the United States is at its highest level in 50 years according to the Census Bureau which uses conservative numbers. The United States is the most economically stratified industrial nation in the world, and inequality is growing faster here than anywhere else.

If the poor have little or no hope of entering the economic mainstream, what has become of them? Young males of color are being imprisoned. While rates of all violent crimes are on the decrease, prison populations are growing at an unprecedented rate. (The main reason for the decrease in violent crime is the decrease in numbers of young men between the ages of 15 and 25, the demographic age/gender group most likely to commit violent crimes.) Most of these young men are imprisoned for non-violent crimes, usually related to illegal drugs. For every black male in a college or university program, there are five black males incarcerated in a federal or state prison. The statistics for Native American young men are even more dismal.

The *prison-industrial complex* is growing by leaps and bounds. Many of these new institutions are being built by private corporations for profit. Increasingly, municipalities are turning the operation of their penal institutions over to private corporations. Again, they are run for profit and with no public accountability. High-tech companies are specializing in surveillance and other prison-related products.

In other areas, the poor are also at a disadvantage. **Public education**, which was championed when business demanded an educated workforce, is on the decline. Those states that rely primarily on property taxes to fund education assure that the students in low-income areas will receive an inferior education. The push for vouchers for private schools (in the name of providing "choice") further undermines the public school system.

Health care for the poor is also compromised. The United States is the only industrialized country without a national health program that ensures universal health care. How did this happen? Joel Albers, a health care researcher, in a talk "The Healthy, Wealthy, and Why's" explains: *The other industrialized countries have powerful labor, social-democratic, or socialist parties, as well as a higher percentage of unionized workers and stronger labor laws. The U.S. has no mass progressive political parties to champion this cause. The unions are organized by trade; they are often fragmented and primarily interested in their own economic interests on a contract-by-contract basis. They have failed to work together or with their communities. Health practitioners themselves are only beginning to unionize.* Keeping the poor disadvantaged and discouraged serves as a domestic control mechanism. The United States, once a beacon of hope to the poor, has virtually abandoned them as the nation's wealth is concentrated in fewer and fewer hands.

THE STEPS:

They represent the barriers between the classes. Although the barriers between the classes are not fixed, they are very effective. The extreme wealth of the elite ruling class is the barrier between it and the professional-managerial class. Their control of the political and educational systems assures that only those people willing to defend the power and privilege of the elite will retain their positions of influence. Thus, they retain control over the professional-managerial class, which in turn controls the classes below them through their interpretation of reality.

The extensive education and training of the professional-managerial class is the barrier between it and the working class. The possibility of movement back-and-forth between these two classes is more likely than between the other classes, yet the advantages of the professional-managerial class discourage this from happening. The professional- managerial class is in a position of authority over the working class and underclass, thus they are very influential in controlling the way the lower classes think and act.

The increased opportunities afforded the working class are the barrier between it and the underclass. These are primarily race-related. Working class antagonism toward the underclass is fueled by their perception that the poor are to blame, not only for their own predicament, but for almost all the woes of the working class, as well. They resent welfare for the poor, but are generally unaware of the massive amounts of tax money (welfare) used to subsidize the incomes of the already extremely wealthy. The working class exercises control over the underclass, in general, by opposing those things that would give the underclass a chance to improve their lot in life. The U.S. class system, invisible and unacknowledged, is extremely effective in protecting the *status quo*.

The next lesson will explain the origin of the Western worldview of progress, how it is sustained and how the elite use it to further their own advantage.

LESSON 7:
THE WESTERN WORLDVIEW AND HOW IT IS SUSTAINED
DISCUSSION QUESTIONS

1. Are you familiar with any worldview other than the Western worldview? How does it differ?

2. Would you define "progress" differently than the ever greater consumption of material goods?

3. Do you feel that neoliberal economic globalization is inevitable? What other direction could progress take?

4. How can the Western worldview, supposedly based on democratic rights, be reconciled with the expression of that worldview, neoliberal economic globalization that categorically denies democratic rights to the majority of the world's citizens?

5. Do you think that economic growth is desirable and essential for human betterment?

6. A huge profit can be made on arms sales to Global South nations. Does this justify their manufacture and sale? What, if any, restrictions should be placed on arms sales to poor countries?

7. Considering the history of European plunder of Global South resources and the effects of the slave trade and colonization, do you think payment of Global South debt owed to Global North lenders is called for, or do you think reparations are due the Global South nations from the Global North nations?

OTHER POINTS OF DISCUSSION

People are not conscious of having a worldview. People born into the Western worldview, or any other worldview for that matter, accept it as the "natural" order of things. It is very difficult to objectively assess a worldview, especially your own. The Western worldview is distinguished by the concept of progress. Since the Western nations have "progressed" further and faster than all other cultures, some Westerners have felt a moral obligation to help those "less fortunate" than themselves—those who have not progressed as far. This sense of moral responsibility is expressed in British author Rudyard Kipling's poem "The White Man's Burden":

> *Take up the White man's burden -*
> *Send forth the best ye breed -*
> *Go bind your sons to exile*
> *To serve your captive's need;*
> *To wait in heavy harness*
> *On fluttered folk and wild -*
> *Your new-caught, sullen peoples,*
> *Half devil and half child.*

In his poem, Kipling is speaking of the Filipinos (whom he describes as "half devil and half child") but he could just as well be describing anyone in the Global South. Dr. David Livingstone, Scottish medical missionary and explorer of Africa, appealed to Europe to bring the three C's to Africa—Civilization, Christianity, and Commerce. These men assume a superiority of Western civilization.

These words of English colonialist Cecil Rhodes blur the line between "helping" and "exploiting" non-Western peoples, in this case, people of southern Africa: *We must find new lands from which we can easily obtain raw materials and at the same time exploit the cheap slave labour that is available from the natives of the colonies. The colonies would also provide a dumping ground for the surplus goods produced in our factories.* Yet, in spite of this directive, Rhodes was considered a great humanitarian for donating much of his vast fortune (made from mining diamonds in southern Africa) to Oxford University for the establishment of Rhodes scholarships.

Closer to home, every school child has learned these famous words from the Declaration of Independence: *We hold these truths to be self-evident, that all men are created equal...* but how many people are aware that the same document describes the Native American population as "merciless Indian savages"? Is one to assume that non-Western "savages" are not equal and therefore, disposable, if they stand in the way of "progress"? The assumption implicit in the Western worldview is that "primitive" ways must give way to Western "progress" despite the horrendous cost that the "primitive" people must pay. U.S. history books and national policy have consistently condoned the U.S. assault on the Native American population as a prerequisite to furthering progress.

LESSON 7: THE WESTERN WORLDVIEW AND HOW IT IS SUSTAINED

LESSON 7: THE WESTERN WORLDVIEW AND HOW IT IS SUSTAINED

SCREEN AND PROJECTION EQUIPMENT:

A worldview is an arbitrarily imposed picture of reality. There are, have been, and will be many different worldviews.

FIGURE CONTROLS THE PROJECTION EQUIPMENT:

The people with the most power in any given society have the ability to control the worldview. Thus, in the West, and increasingly worldwide, it is the U.S. elite. Their perception of reality will be influenced by their unique sense of destiny (that of "democratizing" and "Americanizing" the world), as well as their elite perspective (that they alone have the ability to determine what is in the best interest of all). What they do not   acknowledge   is the adverse effects that this is having on the distribution of global wealth, the environment, human health, human rights, and on real democracy.

IMAGE ON THE SCREEN:

The Western worldview of progress. It sees progress as the avenue to eventually attaining "paradise" on earth. Progress is defined as "the ever greater consumption of material goods made possible through science and technology and accomplished in the most efficient manner".

SPEECH BALLOON:

The U.S.-led Global North elite proclaim the message that the best means of furthering progress is through economic globalization. As they relentlessly pursue this agenda, it is important that they also spread the Western worldview of progress which supports this endeavor.

ITEMS BELOW THE SCREEN:

The reality that sustains the illusion of progress in the Western worldview of progress. The Global North elite have used secrecy and deception to promote the benefits of the Western worldview.

U.S. POSTWAR ECONOMIC PLAN INDICATING THE TRANSFER OF WEALTH FROM THE GLOBAL SOUTH TO THE GLOBAL NORTH:

There are three primary ways that wealth is being transferred from the Global South to the Global North: 1) unfair trade practices, 2) weapon sales and 3) debt repayment.

DISCARDED PAPER IN WASTEBASKET:

Economic globalization is destructive of the natural environment and is detrimental to human health. In their defense of the pursuit of private profit, the proponents of economic globalization fail to recognize, or choose not to recognize, that economic growth and ever greater levels of consumption are unsustainable.

LESSON 7: THE WESTERN WORLDVIEW AND HOW IT IS SUSTAINED

FIGURE STANDS ON PAPER:

While promising that it will eventually benefit everyone, the end result of the corporate-led attempt to create/maintain a system of economic globalization, inspired by the Western worldview of progress, is the crushing of human rights and the negation of democratic principles for the great majority of the world's people.

SCREEN AND PROJECTION EQUIPMENT:

A worldview is an arbitrarily imposed picture of reality. There are, have been, and will be many different worldviews. For example, the Greeks saw history in a way that's exactly opposite to how we perceive it. For them history was a process of continual degradation. Their Golden Age of perfection was in the past, thus history moved from order to chaos. They believed that the best social order was the one that experienced the fewest changes. The Greeks associated greater change and growth with decay and chaos. Their goal, then, was to hand down to the next generation a world as much preserved from "change" as possible. The medieval Christian worldview, which dominated Western Europe throughout the Middle Ages, perceived life in this world as a mere stopover in preparation for the next. Like the Greeks, they saw history as a decaying process. It was seen as an ongoing struggle in which the forces of evil continued to sow chaos and disintegration in the earthly world. Like the Greeks, the medieval concept of history was not one of growth and material gain—the human purpose was not to "achieve things" but to seek salvation.

FIGURE CONTROLS THE PROJECTION EQUIPMENT:

The people with the most power in any given society have the ability to control the worldview. Thus, in the West, and increasingly worldwide, it is the U.S. elite. Their perception of reality will be influenced by their unique sense of destiny (that of "democratizing" and "Americanizing" the world), as well as their elite perspective (that they alone have the ability to determine what is in the best interest of all). What they do not acknowledge is the adverse effects that this is having on the distribution of global wealth, on the environment, on human health, on human rights, and on real democracy.

How did the U.S. elite (as leaders of the Western world) arrive at this position of power? As the breakdown of the feudal system in Europe progressed and money replaced land as wealth, the new class of capitalists gained increasing wealth and power. Those capitalists in nation-states with highly developed navigational skills (England, Spain, Portugal, and France) gained an advantage as they were able to exploit the resources of faraway lands. Their superiority in navigational skills, weaponry, and other advantages they held over the native populations allowed them to establish these lands as colonies. The corporate structure allowed the capitalists political as well as economic power over the colonies.

Industrial efficiency and greater profits for the capitalists were made possible with the invention of the steam engine, the development of mass production, interchangeable parts, and the division of labor. Maximum material output was accomplished in a minimum amount of time with the exertion of a minimum amount of energy, labor, and capital in the process. The most "successful" capitalists became extremely wealthy and powerful. They were the ones who were able to shape and control the new worldview as it emerged and whose successors, the present Global North elite, continue in that role.

IMAGE ON THE SCREEN:

The Western worldview of progress. It sees progress as the avenue to eventually attaining "paradise" on earth. Progress is defined as "the ever greater consumption of material goods made possible through science and technology and accomplished in the most efficient manner". *Jaques Turgot*, a history professor at the Sorbonne in Paris, presented a lecture in 1750 expounding a new concept of world history—that of progress. He heralded the virtue of constant change and movement. He argued that history proceeds in a straight line and that each succeeding stage represents an advance over the preceding one. Thus, history demonstrates an overall advance toward the perfection of life here on earth. This novel concept refuted both the Greek worldview and the medieval Christian worldview. However, the fact that he was neither fired nor excommunicated indicated that European society was ready for change.

The capitalist class encouraged the emerging worldview of progress since it suited their needs perfectly. By the middle of the nineteenth century, this aggressive new class had wrested de facto power from the state and the church, allowing them de jure power. The state was called upon to protect and promote the interests of industrial capitalism, while the church, in order to survive, also gave its blessing to the new order. The *Industrial Revolution*, under the direction of the capitalist classes, started in England (early eighteenth century), and then spread to the rest of Western Europe. Resources obtained from their colonies in the New World and elsewhere fueled the Industrial Revolution while the exploitation of domestic factory workers and slaves from the African continent provided the labor.

Much of *political liberalism*, then gaining prominence, supported the concept of progress that the capitalists espoused. For example, John Locke (1632-1704) had taken it upon himself to discover the "natural" laws that operated in the realm of government and society. He came to the conclusion that self-interest was the sole basis for the establishment of the state. Society must become materialistic and individualistic because reason leads us to conclude that this is the natural order of things. Each individual need only concern himself with the amassing of personal wealth and all society would benefit. People were inherently good—only scarcity and lack of property made then evil. As the wealth of society increased, so would social harmony. Thus, he expounded a philosophy of unlimited expansion and material abundance.

Locke pointed out the benefits of material progress. He saw nature as a vast unproductive wasteland that technology and human labor could transform into useful products. This advance would make society more secure and would result in unlimited progress. Locke saw the purpose of government as being to allow people the freedom to use their new-found power over nature to produce wealth. The social role of the state would be to promote the subjugation of nature so that people might acquire the material prosperity necessary for fulfillment. In Locke's scheme of things the individual is reduced to the self-centered activities of production and consumption to find meaning and purpose in life. *Charles Darwin's On the Origins of the Species* published in 1859 was invoked to prove that the "survival of the fittest"—those best able to maximize their own self-interest and provide for their material needs—was indeed a law of nature. The capitalists declared that progress was therefore inevitable and would inexorably lead to a paradise on earth.

SPEECH BALLOON:

LESSON 7: THE WESTERN WORLDVIEW AND HOW IT IS SUSTAINED

The U.S.-led Global North elite proclaim the message that the best means of furthering progress is through economic globalization. As they relentlessly pursue this agenda, it is important that they also spread the Western worldview of progress that supports this endeavor.

ITEMS BELOW THE SCREEN:

The reality that sustains the *illusion* of progress in the Western worldview of progress. The Global North elite have used secrecy and deception to promote the benefits of the Western worldview. The U.S. goal of *world domination* is usually camouflaged by the rhetoric of "spreading democracy" or some other benevolent action. This elite perspective is revealed in a 1997 book, *The Grand Chessboard: American Primacy and its Geostrategic Imperatives* by Global North elite insider *Zbigniew Brezezinski*. He clearly states what he believes to be the most important imperative of U.S. foreign policy: *It is imperative that no Eurasian challenger emerges, capable of dominating Eurasia and thus of also **challenging America***. Why is it necessary for the U.S. to dominate Eurasia (and by extension, the world)? From Brzezinski's elite viewpoint, the answer is obvious: *America's withdrawal from the world would... produce massive international instability. It would prompt global anarchy.*

U.S. POSTWAR ECONOMIC PLAN INDICATING THE TRANSFER OF WEALTH FROM THE GLOBAL SOUTH TO THE GLOBAL NORTH:

There are three primary ways in which wealth is currently being transferred from the Global South to the Global North. The first is *unfair trade practices*. The nations of the Global North are firmly in control of a system whereby the nations of the Global South provide raw materials and labor at extremely low cost for Global North industries while the Global South nations are forced to buy back "value added" goods from the industrialized nations at inflated prices.

Officially, this system is termed neoliberalism. More commonly, it is referred to as *global "free trade"*, the *free market economy*, or simply the *free market*. Robert W. Mc Chesney defines *neoliberalism* as: *the defining economic paradigm of our time – it refers to the policies and processes whereby a relative handful of private interests are permitted to control as much as possible of social life in order to maximize their personal profit. Associated initially with [Ronald] Reagan and [Margaret] Thatcher, for the past two decades neoliberalism has been the dominant global political economic trend adopted by political parties of the center and much of the traditional left as well as the right. These parties and the policies they enact represent the immediate interests of extremely wealthy investors and less than one thousand large corporations.*

Critics of neoliberalism refer to it as *neocolonialism* or *neoimperialism*. Actually, very little has changed over the last five hundred years. The dictionary contains these two definitions of *imperialism*: *A policy that aims at creating, maintaining, or extending an empire or superstate, comprising many nations and areas, all controlled by a central government.* This definition is what we associate with the word *colonialism* as it was practiced by the Western European nation-states from the fifteenth through the twentieth centuries. The second definition is: *A governmental policy of developing foreign trade and exploiting the raw materials of backward countries through the use of political and Military pressures, without necessarily assuming direct political control of the nation affected.* This definition of imperialism also applies to neoliberalism. The people who promote neoliberalism, not surprisingly, are the people who gain the most benefit from it – the Global North elite. They declare that it is, or will be, beneficial to all parties involved, but in reality, it is responsible for vast amounts of wealth being transferred from the Global South to the Global North.

The second way wealth is being transferred from the Global South to the Global North is through *weapon sales*. U.S.-made weapons have proliferated throughout the world. The U.S. arms industry exports more weapons than all the other arms exporting nations combined. Cooperative Global South governments (cooperative with the Global North elite) use them against their own people to maintain "stability" and to create/maintain a favorable business climate for Western corporations. In the 1980's the U.S. armed virtually any Global South nation or group which claimed to be anti-Communist.

The expansion of *NATO (North Atlantic Treaty Organization)* creates a market for "top-of-the-line" weapons to the new NATO members and also a market in those countries which may have to defend against the NATO weapons. Weapons are sold to regional Global South powers and their potential enemies. This raises the very real possibility that the U.S. will one day have to defend itself against these weapons. Demands are made by the Pentagon for money to develop and produce more effective weapons for our own use. Currently, many national leaders are demanding that the U.S. create a "missile defense shield". It would be virtually useless for its stated purpose of intercepting missiles fired by the so-called "rouge" states or to deter airline hijackers armed with box cutters, but it could be used effectively as an offensive weapon in any part of the world. It would also greatly enrich the arms industry and divert tax dollars away from social needs.

Huge amounts of wealth are being transferred from the Global South to the Global North through unfair trade practices and weapons sales, but the biggest transfer of wealth is through *debt repayment*. It has reached crisis proportions with many poor countries using up to 60% of their national income to service the debt owed to Global North governments and lending institutions. How did the debt crisis come about? The profits from the 1973 *Organization of Petroleum Exporting Countries (OPEC)* hike in oil prices (OPEC had gained control of determining the price of oil) were deposited in Western and Japanese banks. For the most part, this money was used to make non-productive loans to Global South nations. The increase in oil prices contributed to an inflationary spiral, while another hike in oil prices in 1979 increased inflation dramatically. Unprecedented high interest rates were instituted to combat inflation which led to a worldwide recession. This resulted in low commodity prices for exports which the Global South nation's economies were dependent upon. Thus, the debt crisis was the result of a combination of high interest rates and low commodity prices worldwide. Although it was felt in the Global North, especially by family farmers, it devastated the economies in the Global South.

Why were these loans made and who benefited from them? Most of these loans were made in the name of anti-Communism or "development". These included:

- *military expenditures.* The Cold War was still in progress and money for weapons was loaned indiscriminately to non-Communist governments (governments willing to protect Western business interests). This money ended up primarily benefiting Western weapons manufacturers and financial institutions.

- *enrichment of corrupt government officials*. Huge amounts of money were simply pocketed by corrupt, unrepresentative government officials. These men, often dictators, were supported by the West because of their anti-Communist stance.

- *infrastructure for export agriculture and resource extraction*. Roads, railroads, airports, shipping facilities, etc. were built to facilitate export agriculture and resource extraction. This benefited the already wealthy large landowners and others in the elite class as well as the foreign corporations involved.

- *badly designed and ill-conceived large-scale "development" projects*. Again, these projects primarily benefited the elite class and the foreign investors and contractors who financed and built them.

Starting with Mexico in 1982, poor countries around the world began declaring that they had unpayable debt. What should be done about the problem of unpayable debt incurred by poor countries? There were four choices:

1) The banks and other lenders should absorb the loss since many of the loans they made were irresponsible.

2) The people who primarily benefited from the loans should repay them since most of them were extremely wealthy and could easily repay them.

3) The citizens of the rich industrialized countries who made the loans should absorb the lenders' losses through the payment of higher taxes.

4) The citizens of the poor countries who received the loans (but did not benefit from them and may have lost their land and livelihood because of them) should repay them through enforced austerity programs.

It is important to know who had the power to decide how the debt would be repaid or even if the debt, under the prevailing circumstances, should be repaid. The Global North elite, through their respective governments and without public debate, made the decision that *group #4* should repay the debt. They enlisted the aid of the IMF and the World Bank to collect the debt. Restructuring of debt and access to credit for Global South nations was made dependent upon the implementation of *Structural Adjustment Programs (SAPs)*. One of the purposes of SAPs is to free up hard currency to repay foreign debt. They are promoted on the belief that a relatively unregulated free market and private sector are the engines for growth. Supposedly, growth will create new wealth which will eventually "trickle down" and benefit everyone.

Among other things, the SAPs (also known as *austerity measures*) will:

- cut government services to the poor (including education and health care);

- devalue the national currency (resulting in decreased purchasing power);

- reduce real wages and eliminate labor unions;

- reduce or eliminate crop subsidies;

- increase taxes;

- raise interest rates and decrease the availability of credit;

- shift agriculture and industrial production from food staples and basic goods for domestic use to commodities for export;

- privatize public enterprises (which are then sold cheaply to domestic and foreign investors); and

- create incentives to attract foreign capital (this is done by lowering tariffs and dismantling trade and investment regulations).

All of the above policies are detrimental to the poor and beneficial to the wealthy investor class. However, there is no pressure to reduce military spending, because without a strong repressive apparatus, it would be impossible to enforce the policies dictated by the IMF and World Bank. It should be obvious that the SAPs implemented to relieve Global South poverty do not create wealth that "trickles down" but rather, further increase the flow of wealth from the Global South to the Global North.

DISCARDED PAPER IN WASTEBASKET:

Economic globalization is destructive of the natural environment and detrimental to human health. In their defense of the pursuit of private profit, the proponents of economic globalization fail to recognize, or choose not to recognize, that ever increasing economic growth and ever greater levels of consumption are unsustainable. There is only silence regarding this important limitation of economic globalization. Alan Durning in his book *How Much is Enough?* explains why: *The silence is not surprising. Breaking it requires the richest one fifth of the globe to question their own life-styles, to challenge the all-pervasive notion that more is better. For the last 40 years, buying more goods, acquiring more "things" has been the over-riding goal of people in western industrialized countries.*

Former AfD—MN member, Sook Holdridge, in a paper arguing for the adoption of the **Precautionary Principle**[2] asks: *Why do we humans, with all our accumulated knowledge and good intentions, persistently carry on activities that seriously threaten the natural environment and public health?* He answers his rhetorical question by asserting: *We are trapped in archaic thinking. The goals, principles, and systems designed to harness nature, mine "unlimited" resources, and create consumer demand for anything that can be produced have had few dissenters over the centuries.* While there have been few dissenters, there are many promoters. Holdridge continues: *Prevailing thinking is characterized in this 1997 speech by the chairman of the National Chamber of Commerce. He said: "Get the government off the back of business. Remove the barriers to growth and prosperity. Privatize. Globalize. Expand. Jobs depend on it. Progress can't happen without it. And those who don't agree are either backward, ignorant, stagnant or intrusive. In all cases – "un-American".*

2　Precautionary Principle: When an activity raises threats of harm to human health or the environment, precautionary measures should be taken even if some cause and effect relationships are not fully established scientifically. In this context the proponent of an activity, rather than the public, should bear the burden of proof.

LESSON 7: THE WESTERN WORLDVIEW AND HOW IT IS SUSTAINED

It is easy to buy into this formula because it successfully feeds into our insatiable material appetites. But the cycle also continues to devour resources, decimate the earth, and demean humanity. In our drive to succeed, beat the competition, and grow the global economy, humans have destroyed half the earth's rain forests and wetlands crucial to the air we breathe. One fourth of our increasingly impoverished top soil has eroded away in the last 50 years. Aquifers are shrinking rapidly worldwide. And, the exhaust fumes from more and more vehicles and factories are irrefutably leading to a dangerous global warming. Our health is subjected to increasing risks as exploding populations exacerbate these problems. Pesticides and other chemicals are poisoning the air, water, and soil. Researchers say probably 80% of cancer cases have environmental causation. Yet today, less than 10% of the 85,000 chemicals in use have been tested for safety, and we add 2,000 to 3,000 more each year.

Former AfD-MN member, Betsy Barnum, in a talk, "Ecosystems and the global commons: threats to air, land, water, and biodiversity", explains the relationship between corporate ideology/power and threats to the environment. The summary points of her talk are:

- *Corporations view the earth and all of its constituents as resources that are there for the taking, and that they only have value when the marketplace demands the product that is made from them.*

- *Corporations are able to manipulate both public opinion and government policy through money. They mount massive public relations efforts, for example, and contribute to election campaigns to secure a place at the table both for the drafting of domestic environmental legislation and for the negotiating of international treaties designed to address serious global ecological issues like climate change and persistent organic pollutants.*

- *The WTO has codified "profit-only" in what is effectively a world government run by corporations and corporate interests. This organization has the authority to declare illegal any environmental law it deems to be in restraint of trade.*

- *Through their structural adjustment programs and the pressure of the global economy on third world countries to industrialize and develop input-intensive agriculture, the IMF and World Bank have helped create water shortages in poor areas. They have also enforced privatization of public services by for-profit companies.*

FIGURE STANDS ON PAPER:

While promising that it will eventually benefit everyone, the end result of the corporate-led attempt to create/maintain a system of economic globalization, inspired by the Western worldview of progress, is the crushing of human rights and the negation of democratic principles for the great majority of the world's people.

Jim Hightower, in his book *If the Gods Had Meant Us to Vote, They Would Have Given Us Candidates* describes the assault on our democratic institutions by economic globalization as: *a crude bribery system of corporate governance that is becoming as autocratic as anything imagined by King George III and his royally chartered British East India Company, Hudson's Bay Company, and the crown charters that ruled American colonies. Just a few examples:*

- *high-handed CEOs can, by fiat, off several thousand workers from the payroll, thereby jacking up the company's stock price and enriching themselves with tens of millions in stock gains, while the workers and their families are allowed no redress for their grievances;*

- *your bank, insurance company, credit-card firm, HMO, and other corporations can secretly collect the most intimate details of your private life, then use or sell this information in any way they see fit, without even informing you;*

- *imperious biotech corporations can mess dangerously with the very DNA of our food supply for no purpose except to enhance their profits, then force families to be the guinea pigs of their Frankenfood experiments, since there is no labeling of thousands of supermarket items (including baby food) already containing these genetically altered organisms;*

- *conniving corporations routinely extract millions from townspeople as the price of building a factory or sports stadium in their town, then can renege on any pledge of job creation and, on whim, pull up stakes and abandon the town altogether;*

- *haughty HMOs can make decisions that kill you, yet Congress protects them from legal liability and punishment for your death;*

- *"speech" has been perverted to mean money, authorizing corporations and their executives to buy control of the entire political process;*

- *a chemical company can callously pollute our air, water, and food, leading to thousands of deaths, birth defects, and other horrors, yet continue doing business and continue polluting, with no punishment beyond, perhaps, a fine, which it easily absorbs and, in some cases, can deduct from its income taxes as a "cost of doing business";*

- *a handful of media giants have attained absolute control over the content of news and the range of ideas that are broadcast on the public's airwaves, arbitrarily shrinking the democratic debate;*

- *the democratic decisions of a city council, state legislature, or other sovereign government can be arrogantly annulled by corporate action through antidemocratic entities established by NAFTA and the WTO.*

These are the effects that economic globalization is having on people in the world's richest country. The effect that it is having on poor people in poor countries is truly devastating.

The Western worldview of progress which supports economic globalization has nothing to do with real human progress. The illusion of progress in the Global North is possible only because of the transfer of vast amounts of wealth from the Global South to the Global North. It is possible only because the protection of the environment and human health is disregarded and because human rights and democratic principles are sacrificed.

The next lesson will consider the social structures that have been built on the foundation that the Western worldview of progress provides.

LESSON 8:
THE WESTERN SOCIAL STRUCTURES
DISCUSSION QUESTIONS

1. Do you think government has more power to regulate business or that business interests determine what actions government will take?

2. How does the U.S. two-party system stifle opposition to the corporate agenda?

3. Why aren't more voices heard in the televised presidential debates? Who decides access?

4. How do the proponents of capitalism justify the great disparity in wealth it creates? Or do you feel the disparity is justified?

5. In what ways do the mainstream religious institutions support the capitalist economic system?

6. In what ways does the educational system support the capitalist economic system?

7. Do you think a just world can be realized through the existing social structures? Why or why not?

OTHER POINTS OF DISCUSSION

Like the Western worldview of progress, the Western social constructs of democracy and capitalism have become second nature to most U.S. citizens. A tenet of capitalism that has become internalized is the charging of interest on loans—*usury*. An investment company has a television ad that asks the rhetorical question, *You worked hard for your money, shouldn't your money work hard for you?* Investing money wisely is seen as a responsible way to prepare oneself for retirement or for future emergencies. Most people are surprised to learn that charging interest on loans has not always been an accepted practice. In fact, it is a relatively recent one; the change in attitude came about with the rise of capitalism. While usury has come to mean the charging of excessive interest on a loan, in these quotes it means the charging of any amount of interest.

The Greek philosopher Aristotle condemns not only usury, but retail trade as well:

There are two sorts of wealth-getting; one is a part of household management, the other is retail trade; the former is necessary and honorable, while that which consists in exchange is justly censured; for it is unnatural, and a mode by which men gain from one another. **The most hated sort, and with the greatest reason, is usury** (emphasis added) *which makes a gain out of money itself, and not from the natural object of it. For money was intended to be used in exchange, but not to increase at interest.*

And what about the people who practice usury? The Roman statesman Cicero classifies and evaluates the various occupations:

Now in regard to trades and other means of livelihood, which ones are to be considered becoming to a gentleman and which ones are vulgar, we have been taught, in general, as follows. First, those means of livelihood are rejected as undesirable which incur people's ill-will, **as those of the tax-gatherers and usurers** (emphasis added).

Regarding usury, Hebraic law evinced the same condemnation found in the Greco-Roman tradition: *If you lend money to any of my people with you who is poor, you shall not be to him as a creditor; and* **you shall not exact interest from him** (emphasis added) (Exodus 22:25).

The Christian Church consistently condemned usury up until they found it necessary to make concessions to the capitalist class in the sixteenth century. The opinion of Hilary (bishop of Poitiers until his death in A.D. 367) regarding usury is described as follows:

Like his predecessors, he condemns usury – he, like they, means any loan on interest – which takes advantage of the needs of the poor in order to augment their oppression. If those who have resources they do not need are not willing to be generous with them and give them to those in need, they should at least be willing to loan them without expecting to make a profit.

LESSON 8: THE WESTERN SOCIAL STRUCTURES

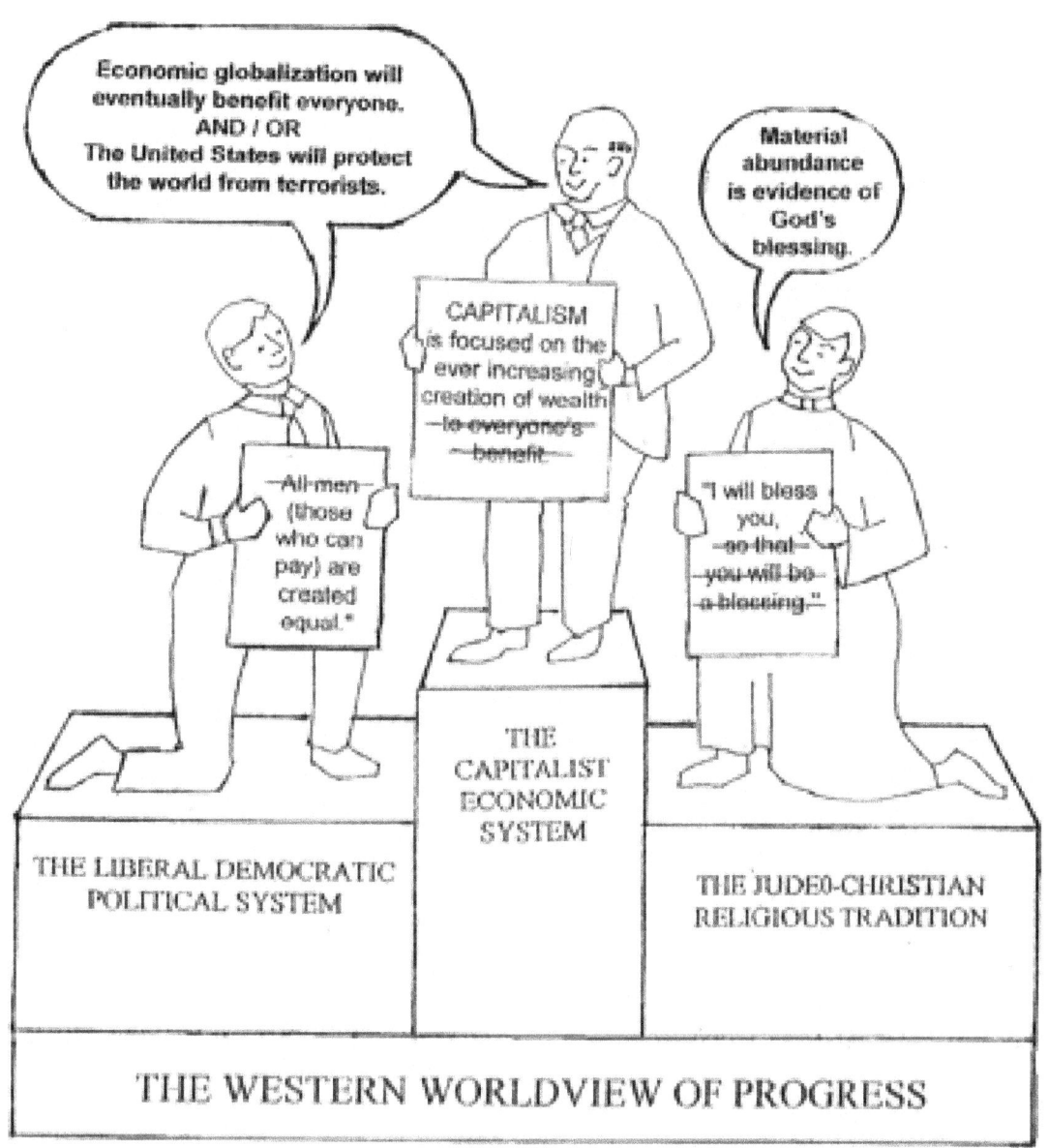

FOUNDATION BENEATH BLOCKS:

The Western worldview of progress supports and legitimizes the Western social structures.

THREE FIGURES ATOP BLOCKS:

The Western social structures consist of the **liberal democratic political system**, the **capitalist economic system**, and the **Judeo-Christian religious tradition**. Since the mid-nineteenth century, wealthy members of the capitalist class have utilized these social structures to consolidate and exercise their power. They are the de facto rulers of the world. In general, they enjoy the support of the Judeo-Christian religious establishment.

FIGURE AND BLOCK ON LEFT:

The liberal democratic political tradition. Although it claims that sovereignty rests in the consent of the governed and that all people are created equal, in practice it serves the needs of the Global North elite.

CENTER FIGURE AND BLOCK:

The capitalist economic system. Capitalism is focused on the ever increasing creation of wealth. Although capitalism has proven beneficial to the capitalist owning class, overall it has been detrimental to the laboring class while it continues to devastate the environment.

FIGURE AND BLOCK ON RIGHT:

The Judeo-Christian religious tradition. Throughout its long history, it has seen material abundance as a sign of God's blessing. However, a parallel tradition insists that justice and peace and a concern for the poor should be its primary concern.

SPEECH BALLOON ON THE LEFT:

The voice of the liberal democratic political system and the capitalist economic system are virtually one and the same. For decades they proclaimed that economic globalization would eventually benefit everyone. However, as evidence to the contrary mounted, and after the dramatic events of September 11, 2001, U.S. elite rhetoric was altered to redefine the U.S. role as that of being "the protector of the world from terrorism" as well.

SPEECH BALLOON ON THE RIGHT:

The Judeo-Christian religious tradition reinforces the message of the liberal democratic political tradition and the capitalist economic system. It declares that material abundance is evidence of God's blessing.

ALTERED MESSAGES ON PLACARDS:

Although the spokespeople for the Western social structures claim that they adhere to the liberal democratic political tradition, that the capitalist economic system will benefit ev-

LESSON 8: THE WESTERN SOCIAL STRUCTURES

eryone, and that they are the purveyors of God's purpose on earth, the deviations they make from these traditions which were intended to ensure equality and justice for all people, in reality, ensure the opposite result - that the Global North elite and their supporters will benefit at the expense of everyone else.

FOUNDATION BENEATH BLOCKS:

The Western worldview of progress supports and legitimizes the Western social structures.

THREE FIGURES ATOP BLOCKS:

The Western social structures consist of the **liberal democratic political system**, the **capitalist economic system**, and the **Judeo-Christian religious tradition**. Since the mid-nineteenth century, wealthy members of the capitalist class have utilized these social structures to consolidate and exercise their power. They are the de facto rulers of the world. In general, they enjoy the support of the Judeo-Christian religious establishment.

FIGURE AND BLOCK ON LEFT:

The liberal democratic political establishment. [Note: In the United States alone, the term liberal has come to identify the philosophy of one branch within the broader liberal political tradition. Liberalism in U.S. politics is associated with advocating relief for the working class, most notably the New Deal programs of the Roosevelt administration and, for a time, the Democratic Party, in general. Since the 1970's the political spectrum has shifted so far to the right that, with the exception of a woman's right to choose, the major policies of the Democratic party and the Republican party, (the conservative branch of liberalism) are virtually identical in spite of seemingly endless rhetoric to the contrary. The political spectrum in the U.S. can be best thought of as being vertical with a top-to-bottom or class structure with both major parties supporting the elite class.] Although the liberal tradition claims that sovereignty rests in the consent of the governed, and that all people are created equal, in practice it serves the needs of the elite class.

Political liberalism began in Europe in the eighteenth century as a reform movement seeking to alleviate the abuses perpetrated on the masses of people by the state and church which exercised arbitrary and autocratic control. It can be defined as the attitude or movement that has as its basic concern the development of personal freedom and social progress. *John Locke* (1632-1704), an Englishman, was an early influential liberal thinker. He argued for popular sovereignty, the right of rebellion against oppression, toleration of religious minorities, and the idea that the state exists to serve its citizens and to guarantee their life, liberty, and property under a constitution. His ideas were echoed in the writings of U.S. founding fathers *Thomas Paine* (1737-1809) and *Thomas Jefferson* (1743-1826) author of the *Declaration of Independence.*

Most early liberals were not democrats and did not believe in universal suffrage. Rather, they looked to the wealthy, educated members of society to govern the masses of the people in the best interest of all. This was the intent of the founding fathers when they wrote and ratified the **U.S. Constitution** (1789). Only white males with sufficient property (about 10% of the population) were given the right to vote. In all fairness to these men, their thinking developed during a time when the majority, if not all, of the kings and popes were autocratic. This was definitely an advance in democratic thinking: power should not reside in a king or pope alone, but rather in the leading citizens. There is a clear class bias in their philosophy, however, as they saw the uneducated masses as unable and/or uninterested in seeking their own freedom and a better society. Eventually, liberalism became associated with the spread of democracy, but only after long and protracted struggles by excluded groups seeking the right to vote.

As suffrage steadily widened in the nineteenth century, many liberals became chiefly concerned about preserving the individual values that they identified with an aristocratic social and political order. They threw their lot in with the *capitalist class* as it steadily gained power and prestige. Liberal political and economic philosophy became one and the same with the ideology of the capitalist class. Their place as social critics and reformers soon was taken by more radical groups such as the socialists. The working class began to suspect that economic liberalism protected the interests of powerful economic groups, particularly manufacturers, and that it encouraged a policy of indifference and even brutality toward the working classes. These classes, which had begun to acquire political status and organized strength, turned to the political parties that were more concerned with their needs — the *socialist* and *labor parties.*

This caused a split in liberalism. While one branch remained true to their now distorted liberal ideals (pro-capitalist), the other branch advocated relief for the working classes in an effort to neutralize the appeal of the socialist and labor parties. They advocated state action to prevent economic monopoly, to abolish poverty, and to secure people against the disabilities of sickness, unemployment, and old age. The branch that opposed this new position saw it as an essential betrayal of liberal (pro-capitalist) ideals. (In the U.S. they would be called conservatives.) Today both branches of liberalism have denied their roots — that of protecting the people from autocratic rulers - since they both support the elite class. In the U.S., political democracy has come to mean being able to cast a vote for one or the other of the candidates of the two major political parties which are both beholden to the elite class and its self-serving agenda.

CENTER FIGURE AND BLOCK:

The capitalist economic system. Capitalism is focused on the ever increasing creation of wealth. Although capitalism has proven beneficial to the capitalist owning class, overall it has been detrimental to the laboring class while it continues to devastate the environment. Capitalism treats everything, including, and especially, nature as a commodity which can and should be sold for a profit. Early on, the popularity of fur led to an onslaught of the beaver population of both Europe and the North American continent. This continued until the near decimation of the species made the practice unprofitable. In like manner, the worldwide whale population suffered the same fate.

Author Ashley Dawson in his book *Extinction* offers a side note to the effects of the fur trade on the indigenous culture of North America: *Over time, the Native American tribes caught up in the fur trade gradually abandoned their subsistent ways of life, becoming integrated into the emerging capitalist world system as specialized laborers working to harvest furs for European traders. In addition to transforming indigenous subsistence culture, the fur trade catalyzed bloody conflicts between Native American tribes, including the so-called Beaver Wars of the mid-*

LESSON 8: THE WESTERN SOCIAL STRUCTURES

17th century, in which the Dutch- and English-backed Iroquois Confederation battled the predominantly Algonquin-speaking tribes of the Great Lakes region, whom the French supported.

Animals weren't the only target of the European capitalists. The fertile lands of the newly acquired colonies were also targeted with no regard for traditional farming practices or the indigenous population. Dawson asks us to consider the plantation system: *The immense diversity of the tropical and semi-tropical lands settled by the Portuguese and Spanish, early implementers of the plantation economy, was dramatically remade as land was turned over to grow a single crop such as sugar. As territories were subjugated and incorporated into European empires and the nascent capitalist system, indigenous agricultural practices that were adapted to the local climate (and consequently highly diverse and resilient) were extirpated. Such well-adapted agricultural practices were replaced by cash crops grown for export to the imperial metropole. Indigenous people were displaced and slaves were imported to work the land, generating a brutal system of hitherto unequalled exploitation based on invented notions of racial difference. In addition to displacing and killing many millions of people, the monocultures of the plantation economy quickly exhausted the land in the colonies, destroying soil fertility, and increasing vulnerability to pests.*

Sometimes the "profit motive" was not the only incentive the capitalists of the United States had in mind when undermining the biodiversity of plant and animal life. The decimation of the bison herds in the United States was meant to destroy the means of existence for the Native Americans of the Great Plains region which it did. The use of Agent Orange, a defoliant, in the Vietnam War served to eliminate "cover" for the supposed enemy, the Viet Cong.

However, as capitalists search for technically more advanced ways to increase their profits, possibly the most detrimental assault of capitalism on the worldwide human population is the patenting of seeds by agribusiness corporations. Seeds, from time immemorial, belonged to the farmers and were saved from year to year and traded freely. However, technology and patent laws favoring the corporations have succeeded in producing seeds which are sterile after one generation and, since patented, are solely owned by the corporations. This requires farmers to purchase seeds annually at whatever price the corporations choose to sell them for.

With climate change and species extinction looming as an existential threat, why isn't something being done on an international level? Dawson explains: *This fatal contradiction of capitalist society has been abundantly evident in the rounds of United Nations-sponsored climate negotiations during the last two decades. During these negotiations, advanced industrial countries such as the United States and Great Britain have refused to reduce their greenhouse gas emissions significantly until developing nations such as China, India, and Brazil offer to cut their emissions as well. The industrializing nations respond by pointing out that their per capita emissions are still far lower than those of the wealthy nations of Europe and North America, and argue that these countries have benefitted from two hundred years of industrial growth, effectively colonizing the atmosphere to the exclusion of formerly colonized nations. As a result of these antagonistic positions, no binding international agreement on emissions reductions has been reached, despite years of desperate pleas from scientists and civil society. It is not simply that the climate and extinction crises have arrived at a uniquely unpropitious moment when neoliberal doctrines of financial deregulation, corporate power, and emaciated governance are hegemonic. Rather, the deadlocked climate negotiations are a reflection of the fundamentally irrational, chaotic, violence-ridden, and ecocidal world system produced by capitalism.*

Dawson asks: *Can capitalist society reform itself sufficiently to cope with the extinction crisis? He concludes: This is not simply unlikely. It is impossible in the long run. Capital essentially tries to grow itself out of its problems. But, as we have seen, the extinction crisis is precisely a product of unchecked, blinkered growth. In such a context, conservation efforts can never be more than a paltry bandage over a gaping would. As laudable as they are, conservation efforts largely fail to address the deep inequalities that capitalism generates, which push the poor to engage in deforestation and other forms of over-exploitation. The neoliberal era has seen much of the global South become increasingly indebted, leading international agencies such as the World Bank to force debtor nations to harvest more trees, mine more minerals, drill for more oil, and generally deplete their natural resources at exponentially greater rates. The result has been a steeply intensifying deterioration in global ecosystems, including a massive increase in the rate of extinction.*

Dawson's conclusion about capitalism is not hopeful: *Capitalism is dependent on the conditions of production that it relentlessly degrades. By fecklessly consuming the environment, capital is figuratively sawing off the tree branch it is sitting on. But it does so because it must: it is a system based on ceaseless accumulation. Capitalists must constantly reinvest their accumulated profits if they are to survive against competitors, driving capital to expand at a compound rate. Every limit to capital's expansion appears as an obstacle that it strives to overcome and fold into a new round of accumulation. But we live on a planet that is self-evidently finite. Capital's logic is consequently that of a cancer cell, growing uncontrollably until it destroys the body that hosts it.*

FIGURE AND BLOCK ON RIGHT:

The Judeo-Christian religious tradition. Throughout its long history, it has seen material abundance as a sign of God's blessing. However, a parallel tradition insists that justice and peace and a concern for the poor should be its primary concern. While the liberal democratic political tradition and the capitalist economic system originated in the eighteenth century, the Judeo-Christian religious tradition is much older. The **Jewish tradition** is rooted in the history of the Jewish people or rather in their interpretation of that history.

The people who were to become the Jews were similar to many other semi-nomadic tribes whose home had been the Arabian Desert, the cradle of Semitic civilization. The favorable political climate at the dawn of the Iron Age (c. 1000 B.C.E.) gave a number of these wandering groups the opportunity to conquer land of their own and to set themselves up as independent nations under a king. Included in this group of small nations were **Israel** and **Judah**. Formerly, as **Hebrew tribes**, some of them had become enslaved in the land of Egypt. Under the leadership of Moses, they escaped from slavery (c. 1290 B.C.E.) into the adjoining wilderness of the Sinai Peninsula. This in itself was unremarkable, but the interpretation Moses placed on these events was anything but. Moses believed that in the Exodus events, their tribal god **Yahweh** (or simply God with a capital G) had chosen the Hebrew tribes to be his covenant people. They eventually came to believe that God was the god of all creation and history and would fulfill his purpose in history through them.

Exactly what that purpose was would be defined differently by different people/groups at different times. At the time of the **United Kingdom** under King David (c. 1000-961 B.C.E.) or shortly thereafter, a writer of a national history declared that God's purpose had been fulfilled in the establishment of the David kingdom and his royal dynasty. This tradition equated God's blessing with national wealth, military power, and a strong king.

But what did it mean, then, when the nations were destroyed and the David line of kings came to an end? (Israel was destroyed in 722 B.C.E. and Judah in 586 B.C.E.) Had God abandoned his covenant people? And what would become of God's purpose in history? The *eighth and seventh century prophets* supplied the answers to these questions. God most certainly had not abandoned his people, but like a loving father had had to punish them for disregarding their covenant obligation. And what was that obligation? They were to demand justice and mercy for the poor just as God had shown mercy on them when he rescued them from slavery in Egypt. According to the prophets God's purpose was not to make of Israel or Judah a mighty nation, but rather to make of them an example to the other nations of a merciful and just society. They were to be a "light to the Gentiles". Thus, a tradition of concern for justice and the welfare of the poor is also an integral part of the Hebrew tradition.

When Judah was restored (538 B.C.E.) during the Persian period (539-336 B.C.E.), the people were determined not to make the mistakes of the past. The scribe Ezra is credited with compiling the ancient laws and traditions into a book known as the *Torah* (thought to be the *Pentateuch*, the first five books of the Hebrew scriptures and the Christian Old Testament) which was to serve as a guide for the people's covenant relationship to God as the priestly class perceived it. Nehemiah was appointed governor (445 B.C.E.) and established the *Law Community* which would define the people's social and religious life. They were to separate themselves from all foreign influence and be a people holy unto God. The *Jewish people/religion* as we know them today, date from this period.

A belief that the *End Times* had arrived and that God would send a *Messiah* (deliverer) to set up God's kingdom on earth engulfed the Jewish people from about 1 B.C.E. to 1 C.E. Rome now ruled the known world and singled out two groups of Jews during this time for persecution. The first was the *Zealot Party* which was militant and called for the violent overthrow of Rome. Open rebellion broke out in 66 C.E. and Rome waged a bitter seven year war against the Jews. The focal point of Jewish faith, the Jerusalem temple, was destroyed in 70 C.E. The struggle resumed again in 132 C.E.; this time the holy city of Jerusalem was destroyed and the Jewish nation effectively came to an end.

The Jews would exist without a homeland or central authority for nearly two thousand years despite being the object of repeated persecutions. Have they been a light to the Gentiles? In his book *The Politics of God*, Hugh J. Schonfield, himself a Jew, gives this judgment of the Jews and the state of Israel: *They have given evidence of a great many aptitudes for individual success in so many branches of knowledge; but in these days when it comes to setting up a state of Israel, what becomes of their wisdom and humanitarianism? They behave as badly, as stupidly, as aggressively as other peoples. It is an insult to mankind to pretend any longer that the Jews as a people have any other interest than in being left to go their own way and in being treated decently and without prejudice.*

The second Jewish group Rome singled out for persecution was more difficult to deal with. Labeled by their detractors as *Christians* (Christ is the Greek translation of the Hebrew term Messiah), they proclaimed throughout the Roman Empire that the Jewish Messiah had come in the person of *Jesus of Nazareth* and that the *New Age* of peace and justice was about to begin. Even though he had been put to death on a Roman cross, his followers believed that God had raised Jesus from the dead, that he had ascended into heaven and would return shortly to rule over his earthly kingdom which, of course, would include a subservient Rome. An anti-Roman movement that staunchly supported the rights of the poor (as these earliest Christians did) could not survive very long in a Roman environment. The transition from enemy of Rome to ally of Rome in less than 300 years is a story too complex and too long to relate here. But obviously, the movement changed much more that the Roman government did. The *gospel* (good news) the church proclaimed was transformed from the expectation of Jesus returning from heaven to set up God's kingdom of peace and justice on *earth* to an apolitical message of personal salvation (spending eternity in *heaven*) made possible through faith in the atoning work of Jesus who was now believed to be God incarnate.

Contributing factors to this radical change included: the turbulent conditions surrounding the Jewish/Roman war (66-73 C.E.) and the destruction of the Jewish nation (132 C.E.), the seemingly indefinite postponement of Jesus' return to earth, the change from a Jewish to a Gentile environment, and the misunderstanding of the apostle Paul's mystical Jewish thought by later Gentile converts. The basic tenets of Christianity have changed very little since the mid-second century, despite numerous divisions within the Christian church. It has remained solidly on the side of the ruling authorities whether *Orthodox, Roman Catholic*, or *Protestant* with very few exceptions. Adhering to the basic belief system of Judaism with its worship of a single male deity (albeit in three persons), the church, while proclaiming a message of sacrificial love and universal brotherhood, was able to justify patriarchy, condone and even sponsor violence, and practice intolerance. *Islam*, although not considered a Western religion, is related to both Judaism and Christianity. Muslims, who likewise worship a single male deity, are also able to justify patriarchy, condone and sponsor violence, and practice intolerance.

The Christian church claims that it has superseded the Jews as God's covenant people. If this is so, then what has happened to God's purpose of bringing peace and justice to the nations? By emphasizing preparation for a life with God beyond death, Christianity tacitly admits that there is little, if any, hope for, or need for, creating a better world order here on earth. It has never identified its mission as such.

SPEECH BALLOON ON THE LEFT:

The voice of the liberal democratic political system and the capitalist economic system are virtually one and the same. For decades, they proclaimed that economic globalization would eventually benefit everyone. However, as evidence to the contrary mounted, and after the dramatic events of September 11, 2001, U.S. elite rhetoric was altered to redefine the U.S role as that of being "the protector of the world from terrorism" as well.

This enabled the U.S. elite, utilizing the doctrine of preemptive war in Afghanistan and Iraq, to advance U.S. corporate interests in the Middle East and Central Asia and to increase the U.S. military presence worldwide. Many aspects of the military were "privatized" with generous contracts awarded to favored corporations. There are presently approximately 1,000 acknowledged U.S. military bases worldwide with more being built. They are, increasingly, being built and maintained by private corporations. These changes mark a shift from a primarily economic imperialism to military imperialism and offer corporations the opportunity to abandon their illegal, scandal-ridden activities of the late 1990s to pursue wealth through a different avenue — munitions and war profiteering.

Chalmers Johnson in his book *The Sorrows of Empire: Militarism, Secrecy, and the End of the Republic* offers this opinion of the damage this change entails: *Our version of unilateralist military imperialism undercuts international institutions, causes trade to dry up, distorts the availability of fi-*

nance, and is environmentally disastrous. While the globalization of the 1990s was premised on cheating the poor and defenseless and on destroying the only physical environment we will ever have, its replacement by American militarism and imperialism is likely to usher in something much worse for developed, developing, and underdeveloped nations alike.

In the United States the symbiosis of politics and corporate/financial interests is evident most clearly at the level of national politics where the two major political parties and their candidates are dependent upon the vast amount of money provided them by major corporations and their financial backers. The same corporations fund both parties to ensure that there will be no chance that their desires go unacknowledged. Third parties that are more responsive to the needs of ordinary people are rigorously denied access to the "system". Even people in power, such as the late U.S. Senator John McCain, admitted that the system is corrupt: *Bribery is the way the system works...The whole system is rotten. Money not only determines who is elected, it determines who runs for office... All of us have been corrupted by the process...We are the defenders of an elaborate influence-peddling scheme in which both parties conspire to stay in office by selling the country to the highest bidder.*

Randy Kehler in a booklet "Political Bribery in the U.S.A", asserts that the only way to ever attain true democracy is "to level the playing field", that is, to take private money out of political campaigns. After enumerating a long list of needed structural changes in the U.S. political system, he continues on to make his point: *Let's be clear. As important as these other systemic changes are, none of them will advance democracy very far if good people still can't compete for public office because they don't have access to big money, and elected officials still can't serve the public good because they are beholden to corporate and other big-money campaign contributors. Replacing privately financed elections with elections based on* **full public financing** *will not only prevent those travesties of democracy from continuing; it will also make it much easier for our elected representatives to enact a host of other needed changes.*

It is important to understand how the capitalist class achieved and continues to hold their power over governments and the effect this has had on historical events. Wealthy international bankers, most notably the Rothschild family of Germany (the U.S. Rockefeller and Morgan families, among others, were their associates), became the financiers of governments and kings. Gary Allen and Larry Abraham in their book, *None Dare Call It Conspiracy*, explain their methodology: *Since the keystone of the international banking empires has been government bonds, it has been in the interest of these international bankers to encourage government debt. The higher the debt the more the interest. Nothing drives government deeply into debt like a war; and it has not been an uncommon practice among international bankers to finance both sides of the bloodiest military conflicts.* The ultimate goal of the international bankers, however, was to gain control of a nation's money supply. This was accomplished as they eventually came to own the central banks of the various European nations as private corporations and were able to maintain their control even after the banks were theoretically socialized. Private ownership of a central bank in the U.S. was not engineered until the passage of the ***Federal Reserve Act*** in 1913.

SPEECH BALLOON ON THE RIGHT:

The Judeo-Christian religious tradition reinforces the message of the liberal democratic political tradition and the capitalist economic system. It declares that material abundance is evidence of God's blessing. While the religious institutions acknowledge their duty to help the poor, they do so by providing charity, but rarely by challenging the system that ensures that the poor remain poor. There are individuals and movements that demand justice for the poor such as *Liberation Theology* in Latin America, but these are routinely silenced, by force, if necessary.

ALTERED MESSAGES ON PLACARDS:

Although the spokespeople for the Western social structures claim that they adhere to the liberal democratic political tradition, that the capitalist economic system will benefit everyone, and that they are the purveyors of God's purpose on earth, the deviations they make from these traditions which were intended to ensure equality and justice for all people, in reality, ensure the opposite result—that the Global North elite will benefit at the expense of everyone else.

The "monied interests"—the Global North elite and the corporations—not only control the electoral process, they also control most of the information we receive. The next lesson will explain the role the corporate-owned mass media plays in furthering the agenda of the Global North elite and the process of economic globalization.

LESSON 9:
THE CORPORATE-OWNED MASS MEDIA
DISCUSSION QUESTIONS

1. Do you think the mass media does a good job in keeping the public informed on important issues?

2. Why are the views of media critics such as Noam Chomsky and Edward S. Herman virtually shut out of the mass media?

3. How has television changed the conduct of presidential campaigns and the composition of the political parties?

4. Media owners are pretty much free to print/air whatever they choose. What are their decisions based on and why?

5. Much of the money raised by political candidates is used to purchase political advertising, especially on television. Do the media have a stake in not supporting campaign finance reform?

6. Are you aware of an ideological bias favoring the status quo in films and television dramas? Or do you feel there is none?

7. What role does the media play in creating an "official enemy"?

OTHER POINTS OF DISCUSSION

[Note: This essay is based on information and quotes from David Cogswell's book *Chomsky for Beginners*.]

There are two fundamentally opposing views in the United States of what democracy is and of what freedom of the press is. The first is: in order for democracy to work, the media has to fulfill two functions. These functions are: 1) the media must report the news fairly, completely, and without bias; and 2) the media must function as a watchdog for the public against abuses of power. This is the view taught in Civics classes and is vigorously promoted by the media itself.

This quote from Supreme Court Justice William Powell typifies this view:

No individual can obtain for himself the information needed for the intelligent discharge of his political responsibilities. By enabling the public to assert meaningful control over the political process, the press performs a crucial function in effecting the societal purpose of the First Amendment. Citizens should have the opportunity to inform themselves, to take part in inquiry and discussion and policy formation, and to advance their programs through political action.

This view is the standard belief in the United States. The alternative view is: in order for democracy to work, the media must persuade the public that the ruling elite govern the country in the public's best interest and it must persuade them to accept the arrangements of the social, economic, and political order in general. The media do not promote this view; in fact, they vigorously perpetuate the myth that the media has a liberal bias and that it is highly critical of business and corporate interests who own the media.

This view was expressed by James Mill: *The media's role is to train the minds of the people to a virtuous attachment to their government.*

In this view, democracy is only for an elite — and the media's job is to "train the minds of the people" to believe in the virtue of these self-same elites who govern (rule) them. This view is more consistent with the ideas of the Founding Fathers as stated by John Jay who said that "those that own the country should run it". Noam Chomsky concludes: *John Jay's maxim is, in fact, the principle on which the Republic was founded and maintained and in its very nature capitalist democracy cannot stray far from this pattern. With this principle in operation, politics becomes an interaction among groups of investors who compete for control of the state. Edward Bernays, a leading figure in the rise of the public relations industry, said that persuasion is the very essence of the democratic process. A leader frequently cannot wait for the people to arrive at even general understanding. Democratic leaders must play their part in engineering consent to socially constructive goals.*

LESSON 9: THE CORPORATE-OWNED MASS MEDIA 111

FIGURE PUTTING PICTURES THROUGH FILTERS:

The Global North elite. They own the mass media and determine what is to be printed, published, and aired. The purpose of the news and the entertainment industry is not to inform the public so that they can become involved in the democratic process, but rather, it is to protect and further the interests of the Global North elite.

TWO PICTURES HELD BY FIGURE:

International and domestic reality. This reality comprises all the raw news available to the media.

PICTURE ON LEFT:

The Global North elite in cooperation with the Global South elite oppress the Global South poor to further their own interests, primarily financial, which is the basis of their power.

PICTURE ON RIGHT:

The U.S. class system assures that the elite class is supported by the professional-managerial class and is subsidized by the labor of the working class and underclass (disadvantaged working class).

"FILTERED" PICTURE:

The picture that the media presents. It bears no resemblance to the above international and domestic reality, but rather, it conforms to the elites' distorted perception of reality as expressed in the Western worldview of progress. Economic globalization is touted as the best means to accomplish progress. Many media personnel share this distorted picture of reality. This transformation of reality, which is essential to the public's acceptance of elite policy, is accomplished through the use of media filters.

THE STACK OF FILTERS:

The five media filters as defined by Noam Chomsky and Edward S. Herman.

FILTER 1:

Money. The great wealth of the owners, the fact that the ownership of the media is concentrated in a few huge corporate hands and the fact that the media corporations, like other corporations, exist only to make a profit.

FILTER 2:

Advertising as their primary source of income.

FILTER 3:

LESSON 9: THE CORPORATE-OWNED MASS MEDIA 113

Reliance on information provided by government, business, and "experts".

FILTER 4:

"Flak" as a means of disciplining the media.

FILTER 5:

"Anti-Communism" as a national religion and control mechanism. (When the Soviet system collapsed, so did Filter 5; see later explanation for U.S. attempts/success in finding a new official enemy.)

Note: Much of the following information is from a book entitled *Chomsky for Beginners* authored by David Cogswell. He, in turn, has relied upon the book *Manufacturing Consent* co-authored by Noam Chomsky and Edward S. Herman.

FIGURE PUTTING PICTURES THROUGH FILTERS:

The Global North elite. They own the mass media and determine what is to be printed, published, and aired. The purpose of the news and the entertainment industry is not to inform the public so that they can become involved in the democratic process, but rather, it is to protect and further the interests of the Global North elite. The elite have a very low opinion of the capabilities of the ordinary citizen to comprehend what is in his/her own best interest.

- *Walter Lippmann* wrote in Public Opinion in 1921: *The common interests largely elude public opinion entirely, and can be managed only by a specialized class whose personal interests reach beyond the locality.*

- *Harold Lasswell* in *The Encyclopedia of Social Sciences* cautioned against believing *democratic dogmatisms about men being the best judges of their own interests*. The elite who designate themselves as rulers must be in a position to impose their will and if social conditions do not permit sufficient force to insure obedience, then a *whole new technique of control, largely through propaganda, is necessary because of the ignorance and superstition of the masses.*

- *Reinhold Niebur* wrote: *Because of the stupidity of the average man, he must be given necessary illusions and emotionally potent oversimplifications instead of the truth.*

- *Historian Thomas Bailey*, arguing to avoid demilitarization after World War II, said: *Because the masses are notoriously short-sighted and generally cannot see danger until it is at their throats, our statesmen are forced to deceive them into an awareness of their own long-run interests. Deception of the people may in fact become increasingly necessary unless we are willing to give our leaders in Washington a freer hand.*

In the Global South, the U.S. often resorts to violence to ensure compliance with U.S. policy. In the U.S. itself, however, a tradition of human rights still stands in the way of a free exercise of governmental force (but is being steadily eroded), so the elite must employ subtler techniques. Having to generally forego the use of force, they must rely on the *"manufacture of consent"*, that is, manipulating public opinion with "necessary illusions". This is accomplished largely through the mass media. Why is it necessary for the elite to manipulate public opinion if they supposedly have the wisdom and beneficence to act in the best interest of all? Very simply, the elite are *not* acting in the best interest of all, but rather, in a narrow class interest—theirs. International and domestic reality must be obscured and replaced with a fabricated picture of reality more palatable to the general public.

TWO PICTURES HELD BY FIGURE:

International and domestic reality. This reality comprises all the raw news available to the media.

PICTURE ON LEFT:

The Global North elite in cooperation with the Global South elite oppress the Global South poor to further their own interests, primarily financial, which is the basis of their power.

PICTURE ON RIGHT:

The U.S. class system assures that the elite class is supported by the professional-managerial class and is subsidized by the labor of the working class and underclass (disadvantaged working class).

"FILTERED" PICTURE:

The picture that the media presents. It bears no resemblance to the above international and domestic reality, but rather, it conforms to the elites' ***distorted perception of reality*** as expressed in the Western worldview of progress. Economic globalization is touted as the best means to further progress. Many media personnel share this distorted picture of reality. This transformation of reality, which is essential to the public's acceptance of elite policy, is accomplished through the use of media filters.

THE STACK OF FILTERS:

The five media filters as defined by ***Noam Chomsky*** and ***Edward S. Herman***. Propaganda is not the media's only function, but it is a large part of it. And, to state the obvious, nothing will appear within the media system that contradicts the purpose of the owners. The question is: How exactly do the owners of the media "guide" the content without being heavy-handed about it? How do they control the content while managing to remain, for all intents and purposes, invisible? Chomsky and Herman explain that this is accomplished through a propaganda model that consists of five filters. These filters effectively remove all the undesirable elements (almost) that may find their way into your living room or into the public consciousness.

FILTER 1:

Money.

The great wealth of the owners, the fact that the ownership of the media is concentrated in a few huge corporate hands and the fact that the media corporations, like other corporations, exist only to make a profit is the first filter. In the early 19th century, a free press took root in England that represented the interests and identity of working people in a way that had been unknown before that time, but by mid-century the small papers had pretty much died out and were replaced by much larger entities. As the market for newspapers grew and the technological requirements of publishing evolved, the cost of competition in that larger market also grew. Ownership is growing increasingly concentrated: In 1982 Ben Bagdikian, author of The Media Monopoly, noted that 50 corporations controlled most of the major media outlets in the U.S. That number has since dwindled to single digits and continues to drop.

The phrase *media of influence* refers to the highest tier of the media in terms of prestige, resources, and coverage. It is made up of a small number of companies who, along with government wire services, define the national news agenda, as well as providing the news itself for most of the lower level media companies. The media of influence are owned by very wealthy people. All but one of the top companies have assets in excess of $1 billion. Centralization of ownership of the top tier of media increased substantially after World War II, with the rise of television and its national networking. This filter eliminates all but a very few extremely wealthy individuals. They decide what "news" is. The owners not only decide what news is, they also have the ability to label the newsmakers and their actions. Important allies, such as Israel, will receive favorable treatment while their enemies will not. For example, the media consistently refer to the Palestinians as "terrorists" and "aggressors" in the Israeli-Palestinian conflict even when describing an incident involving Palestinian children throwing stones at Israeli soldiers in protest of the Israeli occupation of their territories. On the other hand, Israel is seen as "retaliating" when they respond to the stone-throwing with live ammunition or missiles. At home, the media, while lauding U.S. policy, treat citizens critical of that policy in a derogatory manner. An editorial in the Minneapolis *Star Tribune* (June 9, 2000) describes protesters of the IMF and World Bank as *"anarchists"* and their message as *"know-nothing Socialist pap"*. They are accused of *"belittling the indispensable, world-sustaining work of the IMF"*. The media support the interests of the wealthy owners and people like them.

FILTER 2:

Advertising as the primary source of income is the second filter. Before the rise of advertising, the price of a newspaper had to cover the costs of production. But with advertisers to pay the bills, a publication could be marketed at less than the cost to publish it. This put papers that do not sell advertising out of the market. Why would selling advertising distort the news? Advertising distorts the news because it makes a publication more accountable to its advertisers than to its readers. Media with an advertising subsidy can undercut the prices of media without advertising and they can then pick up the market of the low income readers as well. Advertisers learned early on that advertising in publications that cater to the affluent will make them more money for the simple reason that the affluent have more money to spend. Publications that represent the interests and support the world view of the working classes are at a disadvantage in the advertising competition because their readers are of modest means.

U.S. broadcast media programming, as well as print media, is bought and sold by the advertisers. And they are not shy about controlling it. Programs that raise concerns over environmental or human rights issues that are consequences of the corporate system are not likely to be well-received at any network, even on public TV. Television networks know what will sell to their advertisers and what won't. It takes little intelligence to figure out that programs that create doubt over the way big business operates probably won't sell to large corporate sponsors. Sponsors also object to programming that discusses disturbing and complex issues that may disrupt the "buying mood". TV audiences are not thought of as "citizens" but as "consumers". Sponsors want entertainment that will offend the fewest people possible and will create no disturbance. The primary purpose of the media from the standpoint of those who own it is to sell the products and services of their advertisers so that they can continue to sell advertising.

FILTER 3:

Reliance on information provided by government, business, and "experts" is the third filter. In order to fill daily quotas for news material, the institutions of news media need steady reliable sources of news information. Reporters cannot be everywhere at once waiting for news stories to break so they concentrate their activities in places where news is routinely breaking every day, places like the White House, the Pentagon, and the halls of Congress. Big business leaders are also credible sources for news stories. Information from these sources does not have to be checked or backed up; it is deemed credible by virtue of who it comes from. This saves a lot of time, costly research and fact-checking. The news bureaucracies have an affinity with governmental and business bureaucracies and rely on them to satisfy their needs for a steady flow of news at low cost. These sources do not make themselves available to journalists who may print or air a contrary opinion.

Similar forces are in operation on local levels, with city hall and the police department as regular beats. Government bureaucracies cater to the needs of news organizations, creating symbiotic relationships by making the work of gathering news easier, less expensive, government-sanctioned, and corporate-blessed. Besides, if you doubt the "official government version" of the news, you can always consult the experts. Of course, experts can be co-opted by big corporate or government interests who can fund them, sponsor them, or put them on their payrolls.

FILTER 4:

Flak. Flak is an insider's word for negative reactions to media statements in the form of letters, phone calls, petitions, lawsuits, speeches, congressional bills, and other forms of punitive action. The capacity to generate flak that is truly threatening is proportional to power. The powerful can generate flak directly, such as letters or phone calls from the White House to anchormen or producers, demands from the FCC (Federal Communications Commission) to produce documents related to a specific program, or threats from ad agencies or big sponsors to pull advertising or to sue. The powerful can create flak indirectly by complaining against offending journalists to their employers, their media's owners and stockholders, by funding right wing media-monitors and think tanks that can be relied on to attack the offending media, or by funding political campaigns of candidates who support their policies and will take a hard line toward media deviation.

FILTER 5:

Anti-Communism. In 1988 the Soviet Union fell, forcing a rewrite of America's national obsession with anti-Communism as the central noble cause, the one unquestioned value in culture other than making money. Although the United States was founded on revolution, in our time the word revolution has become identified with an evil menace. The revolutions of Russia, China, and Cuba were extremely threatening to the ruling elite because Communism would undermine their superior class status. It became the malevolent presence by which everything was justified. Communism gave the population an enemy against which to mobilize; anti-Communism remained the center of American political ideology for over forty years.

After the fall of the Soviet Union and up until September 11, 2001, there was some confusion from the propaganda experts as to what enemy would be worthy of taking the place of the Evil Empire. On and off again, Saddam Hussein has served the purpose, but a more reliable and malleable image was that of **Islamic fundamentalists** or Middle Easterners in general, who were portrayed as rabid extremists and terrorists as a general cultural trait. The **War on Drugs** also served as a rallying cry so that huge amounts of money could be transferred to "friendly" governments, such as Colombia, to fight counter-insurgency wars against their native populations and for the benefit of Western corporations. A problem that developed with this enemy (illegal drug dealers) was that *both* sides—the insurgent rebels *and* the U.S.-supported Colombian government forces—were involved in the illegal drug trade. The only way to determine who the "good guys" were (in elite parlance) was to understand who was on the side of U.S. business interests (the good guys) and who was fighting for the rights of the native population or simply for their own self-interest apart from U.S. elite interest (the bad guys).

The concept of rogue states such as Libya, North Korea, and Iraq was also utilized. The State Department, however, announced in June, 2000 that it would be retiring that term in favor of the phrase states of concern which means that these states were capable of reforming themselves and, therefore, were not nearly as great a menace as a rogue state which evidently could not reform itself. However, in his January 29, 2002 state-of-the-union message, George W. Bush up-graded (down-graded?) North Korea, Iran, and Iraq to an **"axis of evil"**.

But as of September 11, 2001, a new official enemy was anointed and a "war on terrorism" was declared. President **George W. Bush** has repeatedly stated: *You're either with the civilized world* [the United States and its allies] or *you're with the terrorists*. The mass media lined up in support of the "civilized world". Norman Solomon in an article "Media War Without End" in *Z Magazine* (December 2001) reports: CBS news anchor, Dan Rather, a guest on David Letterman's September 17 show pledged his loyalty to the cause: *George Bush is the president, he makes the decisions. Wherever he wants me to line up, just tell me where. And he'll make the call.*

News Corp magnate Rupert Murdoch, speaking for Fox, promised: "We'll do whatever is our patriotic duty." CNN, owned by the world's largest media conglomerate AOL Time Warner, was eager to present itself as a team player: "In deciding what to air, CNN will consider guidance from appropriate authorities."

"Guidance" from the "appropriate authorities" is exactly what the president's strategists had in mind —brandishing a club without quite needing to swing it. As longtime White House reporter Helen Thomas noted in a column, "To most people, a 'request' to the television networks from the White House in wartime carries with it the weight of a government command. The major networks obviously saw it that way." The country's TV news behemoths snapped to attention and saluted the commander in chief. "I think they gave away a precedent, in effect," said James Naughton, president of the Poynter

Institute for Media Studies. "And now it's going to be hard for them not to do whatever else the government asks."

As far as the Global North elite are concerned, the real enemy is, as it always has been, anyone or anything that stands in the way of their goal of economic globalization. The you're-either-with-us-or-you're-with-the-terrorists-mentality makes anyone or any group that opposes U.S. governmental policy for any reason a "friend of terrorists". The worldwide movement against economic globalization will likely, at some point, be construed as abetting terrorism.

The mass media, following the lead of the government, has the power to designate who is a "terrorist" (enemy) and who is "fighting terrorism" (the civilized world). The constant vilification of official enemies and the assumed benevolence of U.S. actions has had its intended effect on the U.S. public. David Edwards, in an essay circulated by Znet, "The Tale of Two 'Massacres'- Jenin and Racek" describes this phenomenon: *Suffering caused by Western "enemies" is forever highlighted, boosted and vilified. Suffering caused by the West and its "friends" is forever ignored, prettified, explained away and forgotten. The effect of this continuous propaganda is that many people find it literally inconceivable that the West could be doing anything very wrong in the world: We would not bomb a nation of starving civilians without very good reason, because we have always been a good people who do good things. We would not be imposing sanctions on Iraq without good reason, or without ensuring adequate protection for Iraqi civilians, because our leaders are good and decent people with pleasant smiles. We cannot be standing idly by while global warming threatens an unprecedented, perhaps terminal, holocaust within 10 years, because we are good, sane, sensible people.*

This conviction is utterly crucial – the public will not tolerate the mass killing of foreign innocents unless they believe an honorable goal is being served. And so the media – especially the "liberal" media in which people place so much trust – are up to their necks in blood. We live in a world made up of the outrageously rich and powerful few, of the unbearably poor and suffering many. It is a world dominated by rapacious Western corporations legally obliged to pursue the bottom-line and by allied Third World tyrants armed to the teeth with Western weapons. Yet somehow, always, without fail, the media portrays Western violence as moral, humanitarian, and defensive. Editors and journalists do not drop the bombs or pull the triggers, but without their servility to power the public would not be fooled and the slaughter would have to end. If there is to be a way out of the nightmare of history, it will begin with our waking up to the complicity of the corporate mass media in mass murder.

The media filters distort reality and confuse the U.S. public on many important issues besides the identification and vilification of official state "enemies". Michael Parenti in his book *Inventing Reality* lists some of the questions that would help clarify these issues, but that will not be answered in the mass media:

Why are wealth and power so unequally distributed in the United States and between developed and exploited nations?

Why do corporations have so much power and citizens so little?

Why is capitalism in a chronic state of crisis and instability?

Why do unemployment, inflation, and poverty persist? Why is the United States involved in Central America and hostile toward any nation that moves in a noncapitalistic direction?

Increasingly, what the "news" has focused on is crime (except for "white collar"), sensational stories such as the O.J. Simpson murder trial, and tabloid-like stories about celebrities. [Note:

LESSON 9: THE CORPORATE-OWNED MASS MEDIA

The multiple corporate scandals of 2002 are an exception to this general rule. When such stories can no longer be ignored, the media treats the individuals and corporations involved as a few "bad apples" in a basically good system. The dysfunctional system itself is never addressed.] Sporting events, especially professional sports, are reported and hyped disproportionately to any real significance they actually have. Some of the reasons for this is that these types of stories are inexpensive to cover, they entertain (distract) the public, and they in no way threaten the interests of the elite. When real news is reported, there is seldom a hint as to how it might be related to the inequitable distribution of wealth between and within countries or how economic globalization might be impacting the situation.

There is another thing that the mass media promotes: a false history that leaves out the major players and bears little resemblance to reality. The media suppress any inquiry into the role of corporations in the formulation of foreign policy. At times they have to concede that the government does make errors but these generally arise from U.S. naiveté and simpleminded goodness. If a covert operation or other scandal is disclosed, it is treated as an isolated incident, certainly not the norm. The effects U.S. foreign policy has on the ordinary people of the Global South are purposely kept out of view. There is a very good reason why the owners of the media operate in this way: they recognize that the public would not support the actual policies; therefore, it is important to prevent any knowledge or understanding of them.

Most journalists pride themselves on their independence and discernment. How can so many of them arrive at the same misguided point of view? Within the media system, the herd instinct assures that the proper point of view is maintained. Reporters do not have to consciously distort the news. If they adopt the "correct" worldview, they will write as they are supposed to write. Whoever writes for a newspaper must write in the editorial voice of that paper. Whatever deviates too far will be cut out. Those who wish to remain employed, to maintain the prestige of working for an important paper, to keep their employment resumes blemish-free will toe the line.

Nicholas Johnson explains the four stages of the socialization of a journalist: In stage one, the young, dedicated, idealistic reporter goes out and investigates something and writes an expose of the local power guys who also happen to be big advertisers for the newspapers. He comes back and shows it to his editor and the editor says. "No, that's silly. We can't do that. That won't fly." Stage two, he doesn't go out and write it. He gets another idea about something that should be looked into but he goes to talk to the editor first and the editor says, "No, forget it." Stage three, he gets the idea and then he dismisses it himself and says, "That's silly." In stage four, he no longer gets the idea.

Is it fair to accuse the entertainment industry of having the same political bias as journalism? Isn't entertainment, well, just that, entertainment? While there are many people who claim and want us to believe that entertainment is value-free and has no point of view, there are critics such as Erik Barnouw who has concluded that: *popular entertainment is basically propaganda for the status quo.* This is the point of view taken by Michael Parenti in his book *Make-believe Media* in which he states: *I will try to demonstrate...that over the years, films and television programs have propagated images and ideologies that are supportive of imperialism, phobic anticommunism, capitalism, racism, sexism, militarism, authoritarian violence, vigilantism, and anti-working-class attitudes. More specifically, media dramas teach us that:*

- *individual effort is preferable to collective action;*

- *free enterprise is the best economic system in the world;*

- *private monetary gain is a central and worthy objective of life;*

- *affluent professionals are more interesting than blue-collar or ordinary service workers;*

- *all Americans are equal, but some (the underprivileged) must prove themselves worthy of equality;*

- *women and minorities are not really as capable, effective, or interesting as white males;*

- *the police and everyone else should be given a freer hand in combating the large criminal element in the United States, using generous applications of force and violence without too much attention to constitutional rights;*

- *the ills of society are caused by individual malefactors and not by anything in the socioeconomic system;*

- *there are some unworthy persons in our established institutions, but they usually are dealt with and eventually are deprived of their positions of responsibility;*

- *U.S. military force is directed only toward laudable goals, although individuals in the military may sometimes abuse their power;*

- *Western industrial and military might, especially that of the United States, has been a civilizing force for the benefit of "backward" peoples throughout the Third World;*

- *the United States and the entire West have long been threatened from abroad by foreign aggressors, such as Russians, Communist terrorists, and swarthy hordes of savages, and at home by un-American subversives and conspirators. These threats can be eradicated by a vigilant counterintelligence and by sufficient doses of force and violence.*

The Global North elite have the ability to exclude dissenting views from the media, which they do routinely. Antonio Gramsci describes the ideological hegemonic process: *Alternative views are preempted and pushed to the margins of society, rather than censored outright. Hegemony is more effective when oppositional themes are seen as so lacking in validity as to be unworthy of exposure or rebuttal. Thus, the bulk of the public remains unaware and untouched by dissident understandings of past and present reality.*

What is presented by its corporate owners as a "free press" is in reality a powerful force to protect and further the interests of the owners and people like them. Their interests will best be served by promoting the system of economic globalization.

The next lesson explains who/what the enemies of the Western worldview are—both those that are real and those that are manufactured.

LESSON 10:
THREATS TO THE WESTERN WORLD ORDER
— REAL AND MANUFACTURED
DISCUSSION QUESTIONS

1. What are your recollections of the Cold War?

2. How convinced were you that a Soviet-led Communistic takeover of the world was a serious threat to the Western world order?

3. Could the vast amount of money spent on the Cold War and the War on Terror have been used for a better purpose? Or was it justified?

4. Policy-makers seem convinced that they are acting in the best interest of the U.S. public when they deceive them as to the real intent of their policies. Do you agree with this statement?

5. Is the use of force against peaceful demonstrators protesting governmental policies an indication of how threatening dissident ideas are to the power structure?

6. Do you feel that the War on Terror was an appropriate response to the dramatic events of September 11, 2001?

7. Can a system built on deception of U.S. citizens and repression of Global South nations sustain itself indefinitely? What is the alternative? Or is there an alternative?

OTHER POINTS OF DISCUSSION

One of the most shameful episodes of anti-Communism has been the persecution of the church in Latin America. Why were thousands of church workers, including an archbishop and many priests and nuns killed? Because the United States government had identified those who practiced Liberation Theology within the Catholic Church and other denominations as Communists or agents of Communists.

U.S. foreign policy must begin to counter liberation theology as it is utilized in Latin America by the "liberation theology" clergy. Unfortunately, Marxist-Leninist forces have utilized the church as a political weapon against private property and productive capitalism by infiltrating the religious community with ideas that are less Christian than Communist. (The Council for Inter-American Security, in a paper commonly referred to as the Santa Fe Report [1980], which described and set the ideological foreign policy agenda for the Reagan administration.)

Liberation Theology emerged in Latin America in the 1960's as a movement primarily within the Roman Catholic Church in support of the rights of the poor. The church traditionally had supported the status quo and could be counted on to denounce Marxism on the grounds that it is both atheistic and socialistic. However, the Liberation Theologians perceived that the oppression of the poor was due primarily to the structural injustice inherent in the capitalist economic system, which had by now become monopolistic and imperialistic. Thus, their call for "liberation" was for liberation from the global capitalist system which held the poor in bondage. In Cold War thinking, if a person is anti-capitalist, they are automatically pro-Communist, and therefore, are the enemy. The "national security state" — mentality of that era set no limits on what were acceptable means to accomplish the overreaching goal of "containing Communism".

Jack Nelson-Pallmeyer, in his book, *War Against the Poor* quotes a Salvadoran Christian who describes his experience as follows: *By a miracle I am able to tell you the story of my grand crime for which they threatened me with death. They took my son who was 18 years old, shot him, peeled off his skin and cut him into pieces. Then they hung him from a cross in a tree. They cut his testicles off and put them in his mouth. They did this to warn me because I was a celebrator of the word of God. That was my crime. We had to leave because they persecuted the whole land.*

Our crime is to be poor and ask for bread. Here the laws only favor the rich. However, the great majority of people are poor. Those who have jobs are exploited daily in the factories and on the farms. Without land we cannot plant. There is no work. This brings more hunger, more misery. We are without clothes, schools, or jobs. And so we demonstrate. But to speak of justice is to be called a Communist, to ask for bread is subversive. It is a war of extermination. It is a crime to be a Christian and to demand justice. (Salvadoran Campesino and Delegate of the Word, April, 1988)

LESSON 10: THREATS TO THE WESTERN WORLD ORDER 123

LESSON 10: THREATS TO THE WESTERN WORLD ORDER

ERECT FIGURE:

The U.S.-led Global North elite. They have the power to define what threats to the Western world order are—both real and manufactured. A manufactured threat, to be most effective, must be linked to a readily identifiable enemy.

MESSAGE IN GLOBAL NORTH ELITE SPEECH BALLOON:

Following World War II, U.S. policy-planners correctly perceived that the U.S. public would not accept the means they deemed necessary to attain their goal of world domination—the military and political domination of major parts of the world. Thus, they **manufactured** the threat of a Soviet-led Communistic takeover of the world to scare U.S. citizens into the acceptance of elite policies. It was presented as a struggle between the forces of good—the U.S. and its allies who were fighting for peace, prosperity, freedom, and democracy for everyone—against the forces of evil—the Soviet Union and its allies who were atheistic, totalitarian Communists who wanted to conquer the world. However, with the collapse of the Soviet Union, the threat of Communism evaporated. After several largely unsuccessful attempts to manufacture a threat of sufficient magnitude, the devastating events of September 11, 2001 presented the perfect pretext. The new "threat"— **terrorism by Muslim fundamentalists**, for no other reason than that they hated us because of our freedoms—was once again cast as a battle of good versus evil.

PRONE FIGURE STRUGGLING TO GET UP:

The Global South poor are the primary threat to the Western world order. If they were to gain their political and economic independence, economic globalization would crumble and with it, the Western world order and U.S. plans for world domination.

MESSAGE IN GLOBAL NORTH THOUGHT BALLOON:

The Global North elite recognize that the desire of the Global South poor for political and economic independence is the real threat to the Western world order. However, addressing this root cause of Global South dissatisfaction is not considered an option by Global North policy-makers.

GLOBAL NORTH ELITE POINTS AT PRONE FIGURE AND HIS OWN SPEECH BALLOON:

The manufactured threat of a Soviet-led Communistic takeover of the world, and later, terrorism, were used to justify intervention in Global South affairs in order to avert the real threat faced by Western capitalism—the success of Global South nationalistic movements calling for political and economic independence.

MESSAGE IN GLOBAL SOUTH POOR SPEECH BALLOON:

The desire of the Global South poor for political and economic independence from Global North domination has remained constant. What has changed is the manufactured threat used to impose that domination—first, that of a Soviet-led Communistic takeover of the world, and, currently, the threat of Muslim fundamentalist terrorism.

ERECT FIGURE:

The U.S.-led Global North elite. They have the power to define what threats to the Western world order are—both real and manufactured. A threat, to be most effective, must be linked to a readily identifiable enemy. Hugh J. Schonfield in his book *The Politics of God* explains why "enemies" are important to people in power:

What the upholders of power are seeking is not the advent of world community, but the means of retaining the hostile attitudes which keep them in office without being pushed to the point where hostility would result in mutual self-destruction. This is called brinkmanship. While declaiming violently against each other in public, circulating false and malicious propaganda, and working against one another when an opportunity presents itself to gain an advantage, privately it is accepted that power groups have a vested interest in keeping opponents in business.

MESSAGE IN GLOBAL NORTH ELITE SPEECH BALLOON:

Following World War II, U.S. policy-planners correctly perceived that the U.S. public would not accept the means they deemed necessary to attain their goal of world domination - the military and political domination of major parts of the world. Thus, they ***manufactured*** (although there may have been some true believers) the threat of a Soviet-led Communistic takeover of the world to scare U.S. citizens into the acceptance of elite policies. It was presented as a struggle between the forces of good—the U.S. and its allies who were fighting for peace, prosperity, freedom, and democracy for everyone - against the forces of evil—the Soviet Union and its allies who were atheistic, totalitarian Communists who wanted to conquer the world. However, with the collapse of the Soviet Union, the threat of Communism evaporated. After several largely unsuccessful attempts to manufacture a threat of sufficient magnitude, the devastating events of September 11, 2001 presented the perfect pretext. The new "threat"— ***terrorism by Muslim fundamentalists***, for no other reason than that they hated us because of our freedoms—was once again cast as a battle of good versus evil.

Why was the Soviet Union identified as the enemy *par excellence?* Since the **Bolshevik Revolution** (1917) in Russia, elite British and U.S. opinion was obsessively anti-Communist. Their goal was to eliminate the Bolshevik government, since its underlying economic principle was neither capitalist nor feudal and was a system which they believed would encourage class hostility and social revolution. Despite joining forces to defeat Nazi Germany in World War II, the enmity remained between Britain/U.S. and Russia. Following World War II, the problem for U.S. policy-makers was: how to change the image of the Soviet Union from heroic wartime friend to that of a fearsome enemy—an implacable adversary intent on dominating the world. How did they accomplish this? It amounted to "mind control". The policy-makers effectively used the corporate-owned mass media and multiple other public relations ploys to control the public. The public could then control any reluctant law-makers at the ballot box. This system has all the trappings of a free press and democratic elections, but is securely under the control of the ruling elite.

The United States would henceforth be engaged in a *Cold War* with the Soviet Union. To placate people at home and international allies, the United States projected an image of itself as a *benevolent superpower* locked in conflict with the *evil empire* of Communism. The Cold War itself was very real even though the pretext it was based on — the U.S. allegation of a Soviet-led Communistic takeover of the world — was not.

These post-WWII policies were implemented at a very high cost to democratic institutions. To effectively fight the Cold War the *National Security State* was established. The *National Security Act* was passed in 1947 which created the *Central Intelligence Agency (CIA)* which was under the direction of the *National Security Council (NSC)*. The power to control international affairs and the important issues of domestic life became centered in a small circle of national security elite inside the executive branch, completely outside of congressional and democratic control. The assassination of *President Kennedy* (he was considered an outsider by his own NSC) was due, at least in part, to his attempts at rapprochement with the Soviet Union and Cuba. If successful, this would have eliminated the enemies-in-chief created by the U.S. elite.

The CIA was created to gather and analyze intelligence. However, from the beginning it was composed of elites and served their interests. Because of this, covert action was soon added to its repertoire. In a paper entitled "The Origins of the Overclass" Steve Kangas explains: *The CIA has always recruited the nation's elite: millionaire businessmen, Wall Street brokers, members of the national news media, and Ivy League scholars.* What do the CIA and the elite business class have in common? Kangas explains: *International businesses give CIA agents cover, secret funding, top-quality resources, and important contacts in foreign lands. In return, the CIA gives corporations billion-dollar federal contracts (for spy planes, satellites, and other hi-tech spycraft). The CIA also gives businesses a certain amount of protection and privacy from the media and government watchdogs, under the guise of "national security". Finally, the CIA helps American corporations remain dominant in foreign markets, by overthrowing governments hostile to unregulated capitalism and installing puppet regimes whose policies favor American corporations at the expense of their people.* The real purpose of the National Security State was to serve the needs of the elite business class with the Cold War serving as a convenient cover. With the end of the Cold War, however, the CIA continued in its role of serving the interests of the wealthy.

Saul Landau in his book *The National Security State* describes how critics and skeptics of the new Cold War policy were silenced: *Now bearing the generic name **McCarthyism**, the 1947-1955 campaign to silence critics and skeptics of the new cold war policy effectively stopped national debate not only about the means and ends of U.S. foreign policy, but also about what national security actually meant. The word "freedom" sufficed to explain the country's goals and ideals; national security became the catchall for preserving and extending the sphere. "Communism" became the convenient conversation stopper.*

McCarthyism could have been labeled Trumanism. The wave of repression unleashed by the Democratic president from Missouri centered on people who resisted Cold War policies at home and abroad, many of whom made up the left-liberal-labor alliance that fought for the *New Deal* programs of the 1930's. Also targeted were people with access to communication channels — the media and Hollywood. Universities forced professors to sign humiliating loyalty oaths. Even grade school teachers, veterinarians, and librarians were submitted to loyalty tests. Passage of the *Taft-Hartley Act* purged the most militant sectors of organized labor and helped force union leaders to fall into step with the state and business.

Landau summarizes the import of McCarthyism: *The leading intellectuals of the age celebrated Western freedom yet paradoxically built the anti-Communist ideology to a crescendo pitch. The very ideal of the free society, where speech, press, and assembly were fundamental rights, was compromised by the policy that supposedly was meant to preserve it. Dissent from this policy became dangerous. Those who did not buy into it soon became targets and then victims of one of the most lightning and devastating purges in U.S. history.*

But what was the real reason behind the official policy of anti-Communism? Howard Zinn in his book, *Declarations of Independence*, explains: *Behind the absurdities, something serious had been taking place and was still going on — the attempt to shape the American mind so that people would react with automatic anger when they heard the word "Communism", so that they would accept the huge military budgets (which doubled from 1950 to 1970 and then tripled from 1970 to 1980, going from $4o billion in 1950 to over $250 billion in 1980) and so they would accept wars and covert actions if they were aimed at "Communism".*

Anti-Communism has been used to justify the support by the United States of military dictatorships in Chile, the Philippines, Iran, El Salvador, and other places. The need to "stop Communism" was used to justify the invasion of Vietnam and to carry on there a full-scale war in which over a million people died. It was used to justify the bombing of peasant villages, the chemical poisoning of crops, the "search and destroy missions" (such as My Lai), the laying waste of an entire country.

The Cold War has been over for decades, but the need for an official U.S. enemy has persisted. This void was filled by the *War on Terror* following the devastating events of September 11, 2001. Edward Herman in an article, "Nuggets From a Nuthouse" (*Z Magazine*, November 2001) explains what this meant for elite policy planners: *They had been searching desperately since the collapse of the Soviet Union for a new national security threat that would justify a gigantic military establishment and provide a basis for an internal repressive apparatus and limits on dissent. Global terrorism fits the bill beautifully — even better than the Soviet threat because this one is diffuse, hard to identify, with an enemy possible anywhere. The threat is therefore open-ended and paranoia-inducing. They might send missiles or the guy next door might be about to terminate you with extreme prejudice. Perfect. Our material welfare may suffer, our infrastructure may decay, the environment may continue its downward course, vast numbers may die, but we will have lots of National Defense and we are in for exciting times.*

Under these circumstances, one must ask if the 9/11 attacks were entirely fortuitous, or whether elite policy planners may have had a hand in their outcome. The "official account" — that the 9/11 terrorist attacks were a result of intelligence and communications failures — was accepted virtually without question by the U.S. press, the U.S. Congress, and later, by the 9/11 Independent Commission. However, there are a growing number of critics who see the security establishment as taking a "fall" for what they believe was, in reality, part of a long-range strategic plan to further U.S. elite global hegemonic goals. **These critics charge that the U.S. government, at the highest levels, was complicit in allowing, facilitating, and planning (or to some degree, one or more of the three) the 9/11 attacks as part of a larger U.S. elite agenda.** [Note: In this section, I have relied heavily on David Ray

Griffin's book, *The New Pearl Harbor: Disturbing Questions about the Bush Administration and 9/11* in which he summarizes evidence amassed by critics of the official 9/11 account.]

The elite, while internalizing American goodness, accept the rationale that "the end justifies the means" with the "end" being defined as "global stability and protection of Global North elite interests worldwide through U.S. domination". This elite agenda is spelled out clearly in a number of writings, notably Zbigniew Brzezinski's 1997 book, *The Grand Chessboard: American Primacy and Its Geostrategic Imperatives*. Brzezinski (former national security advisor to Democratic president Jimmy Carter) opines that U.S. world domination (in his view, necessary for global stability) is dependent upon the domination of Eurasia which, in turn, is dependent upon the domination of central Asia and Iraq with their vast oil reserves and Afghanistan as the preferred location of an oil pipeline to the south.

How can U.S. domination of Central Asia, Iraq and Afghanistan, Eurasia, and the world be accomplished? This concern is addressed in a document entitled **"Rebuilding America's Defenses: Strategy, Forces, and Resources for a New Century"** published in September 2000 by the **Project for the New American Century (PNAC)**, a neoconservative think tank. This document calls for *"a revolution in military affairs through which a Pax Americana (American Peace) can be more efficiently established."* The center-piece of this "revolution in military affairs" would be a program to weaponize, and hence, dominate space. Indeed, the Bush administration's **National Security Strategy**, published in 2002 states: *"Our best defense is a good offense."* The most important new component of this offense is to be the **"full spectrum dominance"** afforded by complementing the U.S. land, air, and sea forces with a full-fledged space force, the **Space Command**.

The objective of dominating space is clearly identified in the mission statement of another document, **"Vision for 2020"** which reads: *U.S. Space Command – dominating the space dimension of military operations to protect U.S. interests and investments.* Griffin observes: *Its [the U.S. Space Command's] primary purpose, in other words, is not to protect the American homeland, but to protect American investment abroad. It is to dominate space to protect the commercial interests of America's elite class that, according to current projections, over $1 trillion will be required from American taxpayers. The "Vision for 2020" document engages in no sentimental propaganda about the need for the United States to dominate space for the sake of promoting democracy or otherwise serving humanity. Rather, it says candidly, if indiscreetly:* "The globalization of the world economy will continue with a widening between 'haves' and 'have-nots'." *In case anyone misses the point of this document, Griffin paraphrases it: In other words, as America's domination of the world economy increases, the poor will get still poorer while the rich get still richer, and this will make the "have-nots" hate America all the more, so we need to be able to keep them in line.*

Another potential obstacle to implementation of the Space Command is the recommendation that all the other armed forces and the intelligence agencies be subordinate to the Space Command. This recommendation is contained in the report of the **Commission to Assess U.S. National Security, Space Management and Organization**, a commission that was chaired by Donald Rumsfeld shortly before becoming Secretary of Defense in January 2001. (This commission was informally known as the Rumsfeld Commission.)

Both Brzezinski and the PNAC authors of "Rebuilding America's Defenses" (many of who held influential positions in the George W. Bush administration) recognized that the enormous cost of the Space Command could be an obstacle to public acceptance of it. In his book Brzezinski asserts that the public would not be convinced of the necessity of this financial burden *"except in the circumstance of a truly massive and widely perceived direct, external threat."* The PNAC authors, likewise, recognized that the needed transformation in the "revolution in military affair," i.e. the Space Command, would probably come about slowly *"absent some catastrophic and catalyzing event—like a new Pearl Harbor."*

The Rumsfeld Commission report also expressed concern about resistance to its recommendations: *History is replete with instances in which warning signs were ignored and change resisted until an external, "improbable" event forced resistant bureaucracies to take action. The question is whether the U.S. will be wise enough to act responsibly and soon enough to reduce U.S. space vulnerability. Or whether, as in the past,* **a disabling attack against the country and its people—a "Space Pearl Harbor"—will be the only event able to galvanize the nation and cause the U.S. Government to act.** Griffin observes: *We have, accordingly, yet another suggestion by a central figure in the Bush administration that another "Pearl Harbor" may be necessary to "galvanize" the nation.*

Thus, there is ample documentation that people within the Bush administration felt that a ***"space Pearl Harbor attack"*** on the U.S. homeland would be "beneficial" in advancing their agenda by influencing public opinion in support of elite objectives, specifically its plans regarding Afghanistan and Iraq and its desire for massive funding to weaponize space. However, this in itself does not mean that members of the Bush administration and other high-placed officials were complicit in allowing, facilitating, or planning the 9/11 attacks. To make their case for high level complicity, Griffin and the other critics cite the multiple problems inherent in the ***official account of 9/11.***

Addressing one of the major criticisms of the official account - that incompetence caused the hijacked airplanes not to be intercepted by Air Force jets—Griffin quotes Barrie Zwicker, an award-winning Canadian journalist. Zwicker states that there are two possible conclusions that can be reached which would explain why the hijacked planes were not intercepted as per standard operating procedure. (He points out that interception is a routine matter, which occurs well over a hundred times a year.) Zwicker suggests that, rather than incompetence, there were ***"stand down"*** orders given: *In the almost two hours of the total drama not a single US Air Force interceptor* [jet fighter] *turns a wheel until it's too late. Why? Was it total incompetence on the part of aircrews trained and equipped to scramble* [take off as quickly as possible to intercept off-course planes] *in minutes? Simply to ask this question is to find the official narrative frankly implausible. The more questions you pursue, it becomes plausible that there's a different explanation:* **Namely that elements within the top US military, intelligence, and political leadership...are complicit in what happened on September the 11th.**

Note: See the ***ARCHITECTS & ENGINEERS for 9/11 TRUTH*** website for criticism of the official account regarding the collapse of World Trade Center buildings 1, 2, and 7. See the ***Firefighters for 911 Truth*** website for criticism of the official account regarding the forensic investigation (or lack thereof) of those buildings.

The obvious question, of course, is: If US officials were involved in the planning and execution of the terrorist attacks of 9/11, how did they manage to recruit the suicide bombers? Griffin quotes Michel Chossudovsky, a well-respected Canadian academic, who points out the ***"missing link"*** behind 9/11. *The 9-11 terrorists did not act on their own volition. The suicide* *hijackers were instruments in a carefully planned intelligence operation. The evidence confirms that al-Qaeda is supported by Pakistan's ISI [Inter Services Intelligence] and it is amply documented that the ISI owes its existence to the CIA [Central Intelligence Agency]. The money trail - $200,000 used to finance the hijackers—also leads back to the ISI.*

Richard Heinberg, in his book *Powerdown: Options and Actions for a Post-carbon World*, arrives at the same conclusion as Griffin: *[A]fter spending countless hours sifting through the evidence, I find the conclusion inescapable: Persons within the US government had clear foreknowledge of the attacks, and efforts to prevent these attacks were systematically thwarted on orders from higher levels. Many warnings had been received by the US government that a terrorist attack would occur in the week of September 9 — some specifying airliners would be hijacked and that the World Trade Center and Pentagon would be targeted. Then, after the hijackings occurred, no fighter jets were dispatched to intercept the airliners, despite the fact that there was plenty of time for this to have occurred, and that it is standard procedure. There are many other holes in the official version of the events, too numerous to discuss here. And finally, the administration has engaged in public — and largely successful — efforts to prevent or limit any serious inquiry into the 9-11 attacks.* **In short, lines of evidence point to foreknowledge, complicity, and cover up at the top levels of government.**

Griffin notes that: *[T]he three men who have been most identified with advocacy of the US Space Force are also the three figures who would have been most directly involved in promulgating and overseeing a "stand down" order on 9/11, if such was given.* Griffin identifies these men as: (1) **Donald Rumsfeld**, Secretary of Defense, (2) **General Ralph E. Eberhart**, current commander of the Space Force, who in his role as commander of **NORAD** was in charge of air traffic control on 9/11. [NORAD (North American Air Defense Command) is a joint U.S.-Canadian air force command responsible for detecting aircraft and space vehicles deemed a threat to the continental airspace], and (3) **General Richard Myers,** acting chairman of the **Joint Chiefs of Staff** on 9/11, who had previously been head of the US Space Command.

It seems highly unlikely, however, that every single person charged with protecting the continental airspace would stand idly by in the face of multiple commercial airliner hijackings even if a stand down order had been given. It seems much more likely that their collective inaction was a result of the confusion created by multiple **"war game"** exercises being run during the attacks, under the direction of **Vice President Cheney**.

That this scenario—high-level complicity in the 9/11 attacks to gain public acceptance of elite objectives—is beyond serious consideration by the great majority of U.S. citizens speaks to the internalization of "American goodness" and the belief that our leaders always act in good faith and in our best interest. Richard Falk, writing in the introduction to Griffin's book disagrees with this assumption: *There is no excuse at this stage of American development for a posture of political innocence, including an unquestioning acceptance of the good faith of our government. After all, there has been a long history of manipulated public beliefs, especially in matters of war and peace. Historians are in increasing agreement that the facts were manipulated (1) in the explosion of the USS Maine to justify the start of the Spanish-American war (1898), (2) with respect to the Japanese attack on Pearl Harbor to justify the previously unpopular entry into World War II, (3) in the Gulf of Tonkin incident in 1964, used by the White House to justify the dramatic extension of the Vietnam War to North Vietnam, and, most recently, (4) to portray Iraq as harboring a menacing arsenal of weaponry of mass destruction, in order to justify recourse to war in defiance of international law and the United Nations.*

LESSON 10: THREATS TO THE WESTERN WORLD ORDER

PRONE FIGURE STRUGGLING TO GET UP:

The Global South poor. They are the primary threat to the Western world order. If they were to gain their political and economic independence, economic globalization would crumble and with it the Western world order and U.S. plans for world domination. Economic globalization depends on the cheap resources and labor, stable markets, and the lucrative investment opportunities supplied by the Global South. It is necessary for Global North governments to ensure that all of these remain available to Global North business interests

MESSAGE IN GLOBAL NORTH THOUGHT BALLOON:

The Global North elite recognize that the desire of the Global South poor for political and economic independence is the real threat to the Western world order. However, addressing this root cause of Global South dissatisfaction is not considered an option by Global North policy-makers because without control of Global South resources, Global North domination of the Global South could not exist. Of particular importance are the oil reserves of the Middle East. The War on Terror has focused on two nations, neither of which was home to any of the 19 *alleged* September 11 hijackers—Afghanistan and Iraq. However, control of these countries is crucial to Western oil companies and their supporting governments—Afghanistan as a desired pipeline route and Iraq for its easily accessible oil reserves as well as its overall strategic importance in the Middle East and the Caspian region of central Asia. Saudi Arabia, home of 15 of the hijackers, remains untouched. Why? Saudi Arabia is a compliant client state of the U.S., while Afghanistan under the Taliban regime and Iraq under Saddam Hussein chose a path independent of U.S. control, even though the U.S. brought both of these regimes to power. U.S. elite attempts at installing puppet regimes in these two countries are proving much more difficult than anticipated. However, their deception of the U.S. public has proven extremely successful. A majority of U.S. citizens believe that Iraq was complicit in the September 11 attacks (it was not) and that Saddam Hussein had stockpiles of WMD (he did not). The manufactured threat of terrorism is being used to further the elite goals of controlling the oil reserves and maintaining a military presence in the Middle East on its quest for world domination.

GLOBAL NORTH ELITE POINTS AT PRONE FIGURE AND HIS OWN SPEECH BALLOON:

The manufactured threats of a Soviet-led Communistic takeover of the world, and later, terrorism, were used to justify intervention in Global South affairs in order to avert the real threat faced by Western capitalism—the success of Global South nationalistic movements that called for political and economic independence. The elite know that the great majority of U.S. citizens would not approve of the methods that they (the elite) deem necessary to ensure the success of their plan for global hegemony. In order to provide a basis for an internal repressive apparatus and limits on dissent the **USA PATRIOT act (*Uniting and Strengthening America by Providing Appropriate Tools Required to Intercept and Obstruct Terrorism*)** was rushed through Congress October 24, 2001, shortly after the 9/11 tragedy.

MESSAGE IN GLOBAL SOUTH POOR SPEECH BALLOON:

The desire of the Global South poor for political and economic independence from Global North domination has remained constant. What has changed is the manufactured threat to

U.S. national security used to impose that domination—first, that of a Soviet-led Communistic takeover of the world, and, currently, the threat of Muslim fundamentalist terrorism.

The Cold War (and with it the threat of a Soviet-led Communist takeover of the world) had been over for more than a decade before the tragic events of September 11, 2001 ushered in the War on Terror. Why, then, was the U.S. military budget greater than it was during the height of the Cold War? Economic globalization and U.S. world domination demand a global military presence. The failure of economic globalization to provide for even the most basic needs of millions of people in the Global South assures that they will rise up in protest and will have to be subdued forcibly. Also, the people of the Global South are willing to fight against overwhelming odds for the simple right of self-determination.

The final lesson explains that there is an alternative to economic globalization, Global North domination of the Global South, and the Western worldview of progress that supports them and shows how we can go about achieving much needed change.

LESSON 11:
WE HAVE A CHOICE
DISCUSSION QUESTIONS

1. Do you think that the dominator model of society is the human "norm" or an aberration as Riane Eisler suggests? What evidence do you have to support your answer?

2. Is the goal of a sustainable world possible within our current system of economic globalization?

3. Do you think a troubled world demands a strong military or that a strong military demands a troubled world?

4. Many people feel that our current system of economic globalization's reliance on the "free market" can solve society's problem. How would you respond to this assumption?

5. Do you think the goal of a prototype partnership community is attainable?

6. Do you think the transition to a partnership model of society is possible? What do you think is the biggest obstacle?

7. Have these lessons changed your perception of reality? In what way?

OTHER POINTS OF DISCUSSION

For many people, a watershed event has to occur before their "eyes are opened" to the truths that are expressed in these lessons. For former Alliance for Democracy—Minnesota (AfD—MN) member, Sharon Thompson, it was the Gulf War (1991). She quotes from a paper written in 1997 in which she compares her beliefs before and after the war and the feelings of betrayal and anger that this "revelation" evoked:

I looked up an assignment from a Sociology class I had taken at NCC. It is dated 2/27/89, thus it was written prior to the Gulf War. I was looking for the contrast in my thinking before and after the war. The conclusion that I came to is that before the war I clearly saw the problems being created by the conservative backlash to the policies of the 1960's [the topic of the NCC paper], *but was placing the blame for them on the wrong people. As unhappy as I was with the way things were going in 1989 after the promising events of the 1960's, I would have seen the government as simply reacting to the will of the people — I didn't question government policy, rather I saw the American people as being selfish and uncaring about those less fortunate than themselves. I would have seen absolutely no connection between corporate interests and what was happening to poor people in the U.S. and worldwide. I would have judged the media to be impartial with its top priority being to inform the public. In my mind, justice and peace were not a reality because people in general were fallible, not because government policy was wrong or because corporate interests were in conflict with the public interest or because the media would intentionally distort reality to serve its own ends, or rather, it's owner's ends. Now I see these three interrelated elements as the major cause of "social" problems.*

So what happened during the Gulf War to change my decidedly liberal, but very naive views? I firmly believed up until the first bombs were dropped (it was a Wednesday evening — Martin Luther King's birthday) that the U.S. would never again go to war. Hadn't the people spoken during the Vietnam War? I thought we had said, loud and clear, that we did not want to settle our differences through war. I felt betrayed — a trust had been broken. The newspaper article on the U.S. bombing of the Iraqi sanitation plants was the final straw. [She had referred to this in the previous class session.] *The realization that our government was no better than any other government — not even Nazi Germany — finally sank in. How was the Holocaust different from the bombing of sanitation plants in Iraq? The only difference that I could see was in scale and that one was hands-on and the other, hands-off. Both were acts of genocide against innocent victims. I was devastated. I knew something was terribly wrong with our government's policies, even if I had no idea at that time what it was or how it had gotten that way.*

Former AfD-MN member, David Shove, expressed these same feelings of betrayal and anger in response to his learning of U.S. collaboration with Fascist governments before and during World War II: *I was furious to find this out. Betrayed to the roots. Morally raped to the core. All that crap spewed at us in grade school. All that patriotic bullshit when behind it were assholes no different in kind from the assholes we were supposed to go ballistic killing.*

LESSON 11: WE HAVE A CHOICE

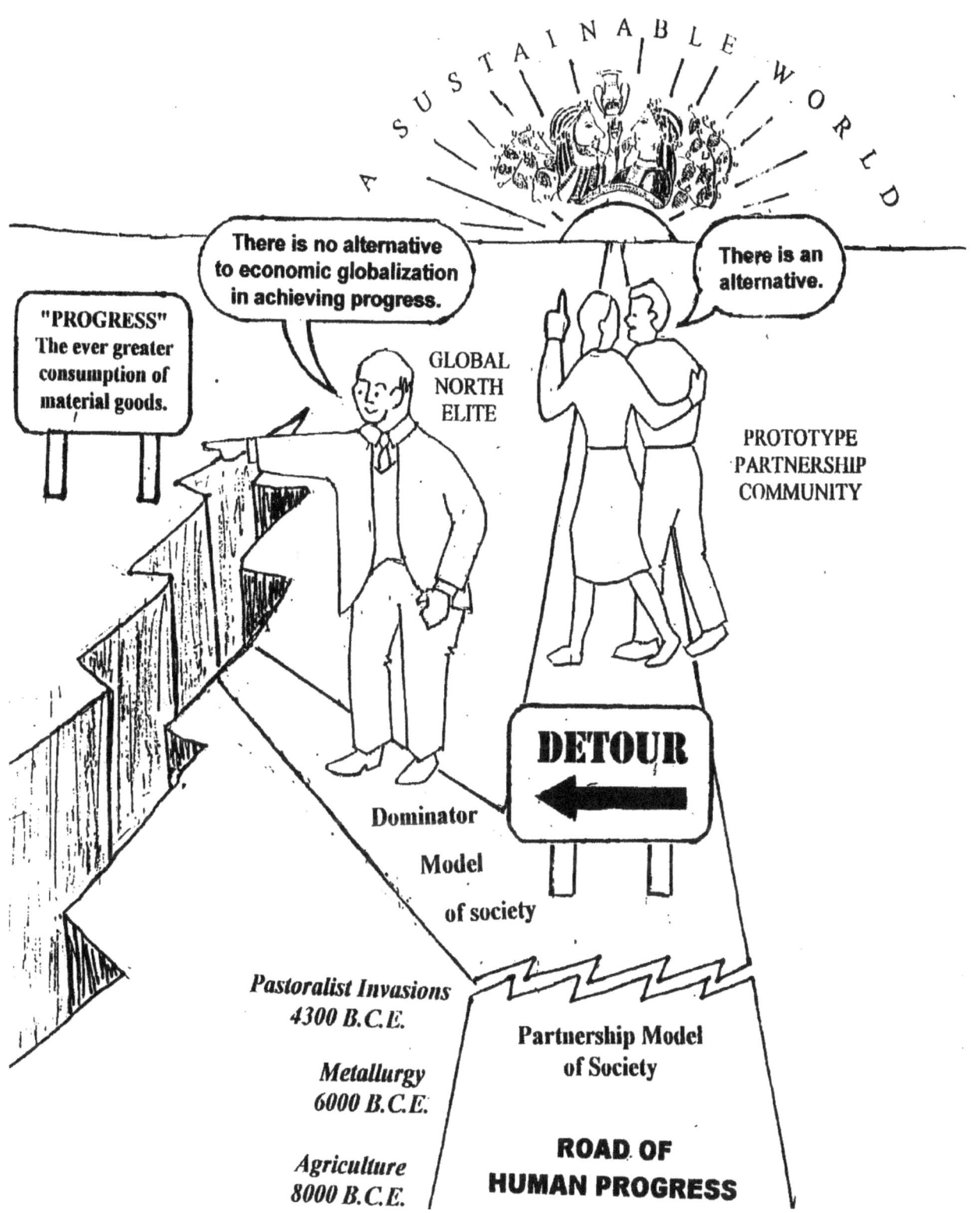

MAIN ROAD AT BOTTOM OF PICTURE:

The road of human progress. Civilization developed during a time when a *"partnership" model of society* was the norm. *Archeological discoveries reveal a long period of peace and prosperity when our social, technological, and cultural evolution moved upward; many thousands of years when all the basic technologies on which civilization is built were developed in societies that were not male dominant, violent, and hierarchic.*

JAGGED LINE, DETOUR SIGN, AND SIDE ROAD:

A major change in how societies were organized occurred following the pastoralist invasions of Europe (c. 4300 B.C.E.) The invaders imposed a *"dominator" model of society* on the partnership communities which disrupted and reversed human progress.

FIGURE ON DETOUR POINTING TO "PROGRESS" SIGN:

The Global North elite. They are the latest manifestation of the "dominators" in a dominator model of society. They are the few who feel entitled to rule the many. They are able to project their version of reality on the rest of humanity and have trivialized human progress to mean "the ever greater consumption of material goods."

MESSAGE IN SPEECH BALLOON:

The message proclaimed by the Global North elite is that there is no alternative to economic globalization in achieving progress. What will the outcome of this policy be?

ROAD TO "PROGRESS" ENDS AT HUGE CHASM:

The inequities inherent in economic globalization and capitalism's profit-motive and demand for economic growth can only lead to further depletion of natural resources, more social, political, and economic dysfunction, and the eventual extinction of human life.

THE REAL ROAD OF HUMAN PROGRESS LEADS TO A SUSTAINABLE WORLD:

There are many individuals and groups who see the delusional nature of the Global North elite's claim that economic globalization will further human progress. The key to furthering human progress is in the attainment of a sustainable world.

FIGURES ON ROAD OF HUMAN PROGRESS:

A sustainable world can only be achieved by humanity's return to a partnership model of society.

FIGURES ON ROAD OF HUMAN PROGRESS POINT TO A SUSTAINABLE WORLD/SPEECH BALLOON:

A *prototype partnership community* that believes there is an alternative to economic globalization. Those people who understand the need for radical change must join together and adopt a partnership model of society in order to create a microcosm of a sustainable world. It would serve as an example and incentive to the rest of humanity and, while the rest of humanity is making the transition to a sustainable world, could serve as a mediator of existing disputes. Then, and only then, will a sustainable world become a reality.

MAIN ROAD AT BOTTOM OF PICTURE:

The road of human progress. Civilization developed during a time when a *"partnership" model of society* was the norm. *Archeological discoveries reveal a long period of peace and prosperity when our social, technological, and cultural evolution moved upward; many thousands of years when all the basic technologies on which civilization is built were developed in societies that were not male dominant, violent, and hierarchic.* (Riane Eisler) In other words, agriculture (c.8000 B.C.E.) metallurgy (c.6000 B.C.E.), pottery, weaving, language, religion, the wheel, architecture, stock breeding, city planning, trade, art, and writing all developed within societies that were cooperative, egalitarian, and non-violent, that is, in a partnership model of society.

JAGGED LINE, DETOUR SIGN, AND SIDE ROAD:

A major change in how societies were organized occurred following the pastoralist invasions of Europe (c.4300 B.C.E.). The invaders imposed a *"dominator" model of society* on the partnership communities which disrupted and reversed human progress. A dominator model of society, in one form or another, has been retained up to the present time. While advances in technology are routinely defined as progress, the two are not the same. Indeed, technology has been used, first and foremost, to create more efficient methods of destruction and domination. This is not human progress at all, but rather its polar opposite.

FIGURE ON DETOUR POINTING TO "PROGRESS" SIGN:

The Global North elite. They are the latest manifestation of the dominators in a dominator model of society—the few who feel entitled to rule the many. The Global North elite are able to project their version of reality on the rest of humanity and they have trivialized human progress to mean "the ever greater consumption of material goods". They maintain their position of dominance through ideological, military, economic, and political control.

MESSAGE IN SPEECH BALLOON:

The message proclaimed by the Global North elite is that there is no alternative to economic globalization in achieving progress. What will the outcome of this policy be?

ROAD TO "PROGRESS" ENDS AT HUGE CHASM:

The inequities inherent in economic globalization and capitalism's profit-motive and demand for economic growth can only lead to further depletion of natural resources, more social, political, and economic dysfunction, greater violence, increased pollution of the environment, climate disruption, species extinction, and the eventual extinction of human life.

Ed Ayres in his book *God's Last Offer: Negotiations for a Sustainable Future* states our options very bluntly: *In effect, we have been presented with an offer. We can continue to focus on guarding ourselves individually, in our gated communities or guarded nations, as long as possible — but well knowing that what we're doing can't go on much longer. Or we can turn our attention to something far more enduring. The offer is to trade our closely guarded security for the larger security of the world we stand on.*

Similarly, the premise of David Korten's book *The Great Turning: From Empire to Earth Community* is: *that we humans stand at a defining moment that presents us with an irrevocable choice. Our collective response will determine how our time is remembered for so long as the human species survives. Will it be remembered as the Great Unraveling or the Great Turning?*

Although concentrating more on energy, Richard Heinberg in his book, *Powerdown: Options and Actions for a Post-carbon World* identifies the root of the problem: *Resource depletion and population pressures are about to catch up with us and no one is prepared. Oil is running out and, if the U.S. continues with current policies, the next decades will be marked by war, economic collapse, and environmental catastrophe.*

Heinberg makes clear, however, that the solution is **not** just to develop alternative energy sources, but rather to **reduce** our demand for energy: *That is why the solution to the problem of oil depletion cannot consist merely of the development of an alternative energy source. Much of our usage of energy goes to facilitate the extraction, transformation, and use of other resources — metals, water, and so on. Without an accompanying demand-side response* [i.e., reducing the demand for energy], *merely increasing the supply of energy to our species will mean the continued depletion of other resources, more competition for those dwindling resources, and an eventual crash. It is our reluctance as a species to undertake demand-side solutions to the ecological dilemma — and not merely our inability to find a suitable substitute for oil — that is leading us toward collapse. Yes, we have to make the transition away from fossil fuels, but we must do so in the context of a concerted effort to reduce the size of our population, the scale of our economic processes, and our impacts upon the biosphere. Otherwise we are merely forestalling the inevitable.* Two of the options Heinberg outlines for industrial societies during the next decades are: (1) **Last One Standing:** *the path of competition for remaining resources;* and (2) **Powerdown:** *the path of cooperation, conservation, and sharing.*

Ashley Dawson in his book *Extinction: A Radical History* concurs with the above writers and specifically cites the capitalist economic system as the culprit: *Ironically, continuing with business as usual is now a recipe for increasingly catastrophic disruption of the basic climatic conditions humanity has enjoyed since the Neolithic Revolution. Inaction is now a recipe for dissolution. Simply in order to retain an environment conducive to the continued existence of our fellow animals, plants, and humans, then, we must transform the root conditions of the climate crisis: the unsustainable capitalist system that is driving the sixth extinction. In sum, the only true conservation is a radical conservation.*

However, Dawson places the blame for the problem on the people who are responsible, not on humanity in general: *Understanding that capitalism is responsible for the lion's share of the sixth extinction helps us avoid the deeply dystopian idea that human beings are innately destructive of the natural world. ... An anti-capitalist perspective also prevents us from attributing ecocide to humanity as a whole. As we have seen, capitalism has unleashed waves of enclosure, imperialism, warfare, and ecocide over the last five hundred years that have benefitted a very small segment of humanity while displacing, immiserating, enslaving, and destroying countless numbers of people, animals, and plants. Everyone is **not** equally responsible for the destruction of nature.*

LESSON 11: WE HAVE A CHOICE

Such a sweeping indictment of an undifferentiated humanity is both historically inaccurate and politically disempowering. Such a perspective offers us no understanding of the structural forces that generate exploitation and ecocide, no sense of how such forces may push the vulnerable to behave in ways that are antithetical to their long-term interest, and no conception of how people in the relatively affluent global North might act in solidarity with those whom Franz Fanon called "the wretched of the earth". Such a perspective is truly hopeless.

Any and all such efforts to work against extinction should be undertaken as acts of environmental solidarity on the part of the peoples of the global North with the true stewards of the planet's biodiversity, the people of the global South. Only in this way can the struggle against extinction help promote not simply forgiveness and reconciliation, but also survival after five hundred years of colonial and imperial ecocide.

The struggle to preserve global biodiversity must be seen as an integral part of a broader fight to challenge an economic and social system based on feckless, suicidal expansion. If, as we have seen, capitalism is based on ceaseless compound growth that is destroying ecosystems the world over, the goal in the rich nations of the global North must be to overturn our present expansionary system by **degrowth**. *Most importantly, nations that have benefitted from burning fossil fuels must radically cut their carbon emissions in order to stem the lurch towards runaway climate chaos that endangers the vast majority of current terrestrial forms of life.*

Rather than false and impractical solutions such as carbon trading and geo-engineering schemes championed by advocates of neoliberal responses to the climate crisis, anti-capitalists should fight for some version of the contraction and convergence approach proposed by the **Global Commons Institute**. *This proposal is based on moving towards a situation in which all nations have the same level of emissions per person (convergence) while contracting them to a level that is sustainable (contraction). A country such as the United States, which has only 5% of the global population, would be allowed no more than 5% of global sustainable emissions. Such a move would represent a dramatic anti-imperialist shift since the US is at present responsible for 25% of carbon emissions.*

The powerful individuals and corporations that control nations like the US are not likely to accept such revolutionary curtailments of the wasteful system that supports them without a struggle. Already there is abundant evidence that they would sooner destroy the planet than let even a modicum of their power slip. Massive fossil fuel corporations such as Exxon, for example, have funded climate change denialism for the past quarter century despite abundant evidence **from their own scientists** *that burning fossil fuels was creating unsustainable environmental conditions.*

What is Dawson's conclusion regarding this dilemma? *We should not expect to negotiate with such destructive entities. Their assets should be seized. Most of these assets, in the form of fossil fuel reserves, cannot be used anyway if we are to avert environmental catastrophe. What remains of these assets should be used to fund a rapid, managed reduction in carbon emissions and a transition to renewable energy generation. These steps should be part of a broader program to transform the current, unsustainable capitalist system that dominates the world into steady state societies founded on principles of equality and environmental justice.*

However, Dawson cautions us: *At present, such revolutionary measures seem completely impractical since most of the media, the political parties, and the repressive power of the state are in the hands of the plutocrats. Yet now, more than ever, we cannot let the present state of affairs determine our horizon of possibility. The terminal crisis of capitalism is no longer a prospect – it is a reality that is breaking across the planet like a series of ferocious interconnected storms. Science tells us that this unprecedented climate turbulence will first wash over tropical, postcolonial nations, where decades of structural adjustment have weakened infrastructure, fed urban destitution, and decimated collective solidarities. Already we are seeing climate change-catalyzed conflicts such as the war in Syria devastate entire societies, generating millions of refugees, thousands of whom have been left in limbo by the refusal of European nations to offer safe harbor. Yet while the global South will be hit first and hardest, the coming waves of climate chaos will wash across the entire globe.*

THE REAL ROAD OF HUMAN PROGRESS LEADS TO A SUSTAINABLE WORLD:

There are many individuals and groups who clearly see the delusional nature of the Global North elite's claim that economic globalization will further human progress. The key to furthering human progress is in the attainment of a *sustainable world*. What exactly is meant by a sustainable world? In a paper "Coming to Terms with Sustainability" the ***Forum for Applied Research and Public Policy*** sums up the essence of sustainability: *In brief, sustainability calls for a dynamic balance among many factors, including the social, cultural, and economic requirements of humankind and the imperative to safeguard the environment. What sustainability seeks is the condition of security for all people.*

FIGURES ON ROAD OF HUMAN PROGRESS:

A sustainable world can only be achieved by humanity's return to a partnership model of society. The decisions that led to a dominator model of society and that sustain it were/are human-made. Decisions that would lead to a partnership model of society can likewise be made. A better world cannot be built by attempting to reform economic globalization or any other dominator system. Piecemeal attempts at reform simply cannot accomplish the major structural changes that are necessary. The elite have successfully co-opted many of the reform movements and regulatory agencies and have neutralized them or used them to their advantage. And if they cannot co-opt them, they have sufficient force to crush them. As the elite are challenged from all quarters (as they will continue to be), they will simply become more secretive, more devious, and more violent.

Riane Eisler in her book, *Sacred Pleasure*, identifies what is at the very root of the human problem: *For what we are beginning to wake up to today, as if from a long drugged sleep, is that we have for millennia structured our social institutions and systems of values precisely in ways that serve to block, distort, and pervert our enormous human yearning for loving connections. We see this all too hideously in the carnage in our world, unrelenting and unremitting now for almost five thousand years.*

The elusive, but obvious, answer to the human predicament is that we must return to a partnership model of society. We must return to our roots and once again relate to each other in ways that celebrate our unique human capacity to create and to express compassion, empathy, and love for each other and the earth.

The biggest hurdle we face may well be dispelling the belief "that things have always been this way"—that human societies have always been characterized by domination, a hierarchical social structure, and violence. Fossil remains suggest that *Homo Sapiens* appeared up to 250,000 years ago. The appearance of *Homo Sapiens Sapiens*, our own sub-species, dates back 37,000 years. The first pastoralist invasions that brought the dominator model of society to

Europe date back only 5,000 years. The fact that the human species survived and thrived for over 30,000 years in a partnership model of society should refute the contention that the norms of a dominator society are "human nature". On the contrary, the dominator model of society should be seen as an aberration, a horrible, but temporary, set-back on the long road of human progress. As intractable as world conditions appear to be with a tiny class of powerful elite decreeing that the world be divided into a rich, powerful Global North and a poor, powerless Global South and that wealth and power should continue to flow to the already rich and powerful, there is still abundant reason for hope.

Frances Moore Lappe in her book *Hope's Edge* echoes Eisler's thesis: *The dominant culture — the materialism, the brutality, the isolation, the destruction, the polarization — is the great aberration, arising in a mere blink of historical time.* To understand our basic make-up she suggests we have to look backwards: *This vast expanse of time — the 99 percent of our species' existence during which we lived in small groups, our sustenance coming from gathered plants and hunted animals — is crucial scientists tell us. Whatever genes shape us today we got long before the advent of agriculture.* She then asks: *So what **were** we like during most of our evolution?* She quotes anthropologist William Ury as he describes the long hunter-gatherer period which he suggests may have been the only one sustainable successful way of life: *The key to its success lay in our ancestors' highly developed ability to cooperate. A more fitting name for our species than the "killer ape" would be the "cooperative ape".*

Lappe and her daughter Anna find it hard to imagine how our species could have survived without the twin needs of effectiveness (to be active and accomplish something) and for connection expressed in cooperation. Lappe opines: *If we're right, then, we must deny our deepest selves when we allow ourselves to be reduced to passive consumers, acquiescing to a world we feel we've never chosen.*

What are the consequences of allowing accumulation and self-centeredness to become the substitute for effectiveness and community? Lappe cites the work of another expert: *When anthropologist Ruth Benedict surveyed her life's work and asked the biggest question — why some societies have been effective and peaceful while others are plagued by conflict — she discovered something we [Lappe and Anna] think is pretty telling. Weighing multiple variables, Benedict finally came to see that only one aspect of these cultures consistently distinguished them. In the more conflictive cultures, individuals gained prestige by accumulating goods or acting in other ways benefiting themselves alone, whereas in the better-functioning cultures, the status of individuals rose or fell according to their contribution to the whole.*

Lappe suggests that we need a new "mental map" or belief system. She asks: *Why have we, as societies, created that which as individuals we abhor — a belief system that allows people to tolerate day in and day out, for example, the devastation of nature and other species as well as the starvation and early deaths of millions of innocent people, and allows them even to benefit — in cheap food, fuel, and finery — from the poverty that so stunts and shortens those other lives?* She then reminds us: *Economic life is not about our relationships to things — like land or houses or hair dryers. It's about our relationships with each other, what norms and expectations we hold and honor. What we see today — economic life as a distinct realm governed by the market — emerged in a blink of historical time. Throughout the sweep of human history, economic life was embedded in a web of family and community relationships, in culture and nature. Our past is the key to our future.* Liberated from the stultifying misconception that the norms of a dominator society are "human nature", we can begin to undo the tragic consequences of the last 5,000 years as we begin to make the transition from a dominator model of society **back to** a partnership model.

Riane Eisler asks: *Will we succeed in this extraordinary chapter of our human adventure in forging new paths for ourselves and our children, in which power is no longer equated with destruction and conquest – be it in war or the war of the sexes – but with creativity and caring, with those powers that are our species' unique evolutionary gifts?* Eisler's confidence lies in our possession of those traits which are uniquely human. *So what we ultimately have going for us is the awakening consciousness of a species struggling to survive. And what we also have going for us is our enormous human creativity: the unique capacity of a species struggling to realize its highest potentials, especially our great human potentials for love, for creating ever new institutional and mythical forms.*

FIGURES ON ROAD OF HUMAN PROGRESS POINT TO A SUSTAINABLE WORLD/SPEECH BALLOON:

A *prototype partnership community* that believes there is an alternative to economic globalization. Those people who understand the need for fundamental change must join together in a partnership model of society in order to create a microcosm of a sustainable world. It would serve as an example and incentive to the rest of humanity and, while the rest of humanity is making the transition to a sustainable world, it could serve as a neutral mediator of existing disputes. Then, and only then, will a sustainable world become a reality. In a sustainable world, the people in partnership can cooperate to attain their own good, the good of the human family, and the good of the earth which they are intimately a part of.

The good news is we don't have to start from scratch. There is much in Western culture that was *intended* to create a society built on "liberty, equality, and fraternity" – all which are partnership values. However, that promise has never been fully realized. While the French and American revolutions started the process that brought an end to "*the divine right of kings*", it began the process that issued in "*the divine right of capital*" and with it the new Golden Rule – he, who has the gold, rules.

The ideals of the *Enlightenment*, at long last, have to become reality. We can reclaim the promise that sovereignty rests in the consent of the governed and that all people are created equal. The idea that the leading citizens were best able to determine what was in the common good of all was a big step forward from the autocratic rule of monarchs and clerical hierarchies. However, the simultaneous rise of capitalism with political liberalism preempted any chance that this system might have had for benefiting the common people.

The idea of democracy, almost universally accepted, must be finally realized. The elite definition of "democracy" leaves much to be desired. The elite have never relinquished their hold on power despite their having embraced what they loftily proclaim as a democratic process. Social democratic governments have attempted to soften the harsh edges of capitalist rule, but the social safety nets erected to that end, are steadily being broken down.

The ultimate political goal of the proponents of economic globalization is to usurp the role that governments have traditionally played in the nation-states. If they accomplish this, then a pretense at democratic governance won't even be necessary. Jacques Attali, former president of the European Bank for Reconstruction and Development, in the summer 2000 edition of "Foreign Policy" made this prediction: *Eventually, democracy will fade away, having been re-*

placed by market mechanisms and corruption. The market economy will rule every element of public life, from police protection, justice, education, and health to the very air we breathe. Under such circumstances, Western civilization itself is bound to collapse.

Economic globalism must give way to small, sustainable, local economies that meet the needs (but not the unnecessary wants) of all. The spirit of the prophetic tradition within the Judeo-Christian religious tradition with its demand for justice and its concern for the less fortunate must be reclaimed. Other religious traditions as well as secular philosophies espouse these ideals also. It would also be helpful to rediscover the ancient religious thought of the partnership communities which saw the earth as a life-generating and nurturing "mother" and who valued the "feminine" traits of caring and compassion.

All like-minded people, worldwide, must unite with one voice and in cooperative action to provide an alternative to the badly diseased system of economic globalization, the Western worldview and the social structures it supports, and the dominator model of society which underlies it all.

The time has come to create a **prototype partnership community** that can work out in detail, on a small scale, the political, economic, and social expression of a truly sustainable society. As in a healthy living organism, each individual would still work in his/her own special interest area within his/her own community (the cellular level) but also would become part of a larger, easily-identifiable worldwide organization (the organism level) whose purpose is to speak and work for the benefit of all peoples and the planet we call home. If this enterprise fails on the small scale with people who are committed to its success, how can it possibly be successful on the large scale? To ask the wrong people (the Global North elite) to do the right thing (create a sustainable world) is doomed to certain failure.

Hugh Schonfield in his 1970 book *The Politics of God* foresaw such an organization coming into being: *Perfection is not to be looked for under physical and temporal conditions. Yet it could be possible for there to be very great improvement, and for some part of humanity to progress so much that it would be able to help and influence the majority. It could be possible for a nucleus of more advanced persons to initiate a further stage of evolution and give rise to a race approximating much more closely to the ideals humanity has cherished.*

This group would act as the social immune system for humankind, alerting the body to the dangers posed by the extension of economic globalization and the dominator model of society, in general. Once the body recognizes the malignant nature of the dominator model of society that it has lived under for so long, it can respond and restore itself to health. There is no reason why the human race, having adopted the partnership model of society, cannot solve its multiple problems democratically and nonviolently. With the good of the individual, the human family, and the environment as a goal (sustainability) rather than the enrichment of a parasitic few at the expense of the many while the environment is being ravaged (malignancy), human society can truly make progress.

This transition is not only possible, but I believe, inevitable. However, like Dr. Schonfield I believe the prerequisite first step is the formation of a world-encompassing prototype partnership community that can model the sustainable world that we envision. It would be guided by the seven Principles of the Mondcivitan (World Citizen) Republic: *No-one is an en-*

emy; No-one is a Foreigner, Service to All; Complete Impartiality; Work for Peace; True Democracy; and Equality and Justice.

As U. S. citizens, we no longer have the luxury of thinking that we can "make America great again" or that electing "the lesser of two evils" is a viable option. We must look for a solution outside of the corporate-controlled two-party system. We simply cannot expect the people who created the problem to solve the problem. Most importantly, the solution must encompass the entire globe, both people and the environment. We must acknowledge that there is but one human race, with all people deserving of respect and dignity and that it is our responsibility to care for and nurture planet Earth. It is up to us who believe that a new world is possible to create that new world. The time is short; we must act now. We *do* have a choice. **Let's just do it!**

WE HAVE A CHOICE: LET'S JUST DO IT

WORKS CITED

Suggested readings are indicated by an asterisk (*).

BOOKS

Allen, Gary and Larry Abraham
    None Dare Call It Conspiracy
Aristotle
    Pol. 1258a-b
Ayres, Ed
    God's Last Offer
Berrigan, Philip
    **Fighting the Lamb's War*
Berry, Thomas
    **The Great Work*
Blum, William
    **Rogue State*
Brezezinski, Zbigniew
    The Grand Chessboard: American Primacy and its Geostrategic Imperatives
Cicero
    De off. 1.42, LCL
Cogswell, David
    **Chomsky for Beginners*
Dawson, Ashley
    **Extinction: A Radical History*
Diamond, Jerad
    **Guns, Germs, and Steel*
Durning, Alan
    **How Much is Enough?*
Eisler, Riane
    **The Chalice and the Blade*
    Sacred Pleasure
Gibson, Donald
    **The Kennedy Assassination Cover-up*
Griffin, David Ray
    **The New Pearl Harbor*
Heinberg, Richard
    **Powerdown: Options and Actions for a Post-carbon World*
Hightower, Jim
    **If the God's Had Meant Us to Vote, They Would Have   Given Us Candidates*
Hilary
    In Psalm 14,15, PL
Johnson, Chalmers
    **The Sorrows of Empire: Militarism, Secrecy, and the End of   the Republic*
Joseph, Peter
    **The New Human Rights Movement: Reinventing the   Economy to End Oppression*
Kinzer, Stephen
    **Overthrow*
Korton, David
    **The Post-Corporate World*

The Great Turning: From Empire to Earth Community
Landau, Saul
    The National Security State
Lappe, Frances Moore and Anna Lappe
    Hope's Edge
Loewen, James W.
    Lies My Teachers Told Me
MacLain, Nancy
    Democracy in Chains
Mahajan, Ruhul
    The New Crusade: America's War on Terrorism
Mandela, Nelson
    Long Walk to Freedom
Mayer, Jane
    Dark Money
McChesney, Robert
    Introduction to *Profit Over People: Neoliberalism and Global Order* (authored by Noam Chomsky)
McMurtry, John
    The Cancer Stage of Capitalism
Miller, Peter R. and John Shoeffel (editors)
    Understanding Power: The Indispensable Chomsky
Nelson-Pallmeyer, Jack
    Hunger for Justice
    War Against the Poor
Parenti, Michael
    Democracy for the Few
    Inventing Reality
    Make-believe Media
Quigley, Carroll
    Tragedy and Hope
Rifkin, Jeremy
    The End of Work
Schonfield, Hugh J.
    The Politics of God
Virgil
    Aenic VI, translated by C. Day Lewis
Wolff, Richard D.
    Capitalism Hits the Fan
Zinn, Howard
    Declarations of Independence

BOOKS NOT QUOTED DIRECTLY

Black, Eric
    *Rethinking the Cold War
Draffan, George
    *The Elite Consensus: A Guide to the Institutions of Global Power
Ehrenreich, Barbara
    Fear of Falling
Rifkin, Jeremy
    Entropy

WORKS CITED

MAGAZINE AND ONLINE ARTICLES

Attali, Jaques
    Foreign Policy (Summer 2001)
Breslow, Jason M.
    "Investigation Finds Exxon Ignored Its Own Early Climate Change Warnings" (9/9/15)
Bucheit, Paul
    "Unsure About Socialism? Here's More Evidence That Capitalism is Killing America" (3/14/16)
Goldsmith, Teddy
    *"Poverty—The Child of Progress" *The Ecologist* (July/August 2001)
Harvey, Fiona
    "Eat less meat to avoid dangerous global warming, scientists say" *The Guardian (9/9/15)*
Herman, Edward
    *"Nuggets From a Nuthouse" *Z Magazine* (November 2001)
The Huffington Post (4-8-16)
    Wendell Potter
Jung, Soya
    "Neoliberals and Neocons: What's the Difference and Why Should I Care?" *Race Files (11/27/12)*
Kellman, Peter
    "Labor Organizing and Freedom of Association" *Rachel's Environment and Health Weekly* (#698 May 25,   2000)
Lasn, Kalle and Tom Liacas
    "1600-1886: The Birth of the Corporate 'I'" *Adbusters* (#31 August / September 2000)
Makwana, Rajesh
    "Neoliberalism and economic globalization" *Share the World's Resources (11/23/06)*
Savedge, Jenn
    "What is Climate Change?" (1/24/16)
Solomon, Norman
    *"Media War Without End" *Z Magazine* (December   2001)

SPEECHES

Albers, Joel
    "The Healthy, Wealthy, and Why's" presented at St.   Paul Public Schools' continuing education class   *Globalization, Corporatization, and You*
Barnum, Betsy
    "Ecosystems and the Global Commons: Threats to Air,   Land, Water, and Biodiversity" presented at St. Paul   Public Schools' continuing education class *Globalization,   Corporatization, and You*
Johnson, Lyndon
    Addressing the National Press Club (1964)
Johnson, U. Alexis
    Addressing the Economic Club of Detroit (1963)
Morgenthau, Henry
    Addressing the UN Monetary and Financial   Conference (1944)
Parenti, Michael
    "The Hidden Ideology of the Mass Media" University   of Vermont (4/9/97)
Rockefeller, David
    Addressing the Bilderberg meeting (June, 1991)
Shiva, Vandana
    (3/26/01)

NEWSPAPERS

Roy, Arhundhati
    London Guardian (9/9/01)
Friedman, Thomas

New York Times (3/10/99)
Jensen, Robert
   "Corporate Power is the Enemy of our Democracy"
   Long Island NY Newsday Minneapolis Star Tribune

OTHER

Apex Press
   "In Whose Service?" (pamphlet)
   Attali, Jaques
   "Foreign Policy Summer 2001" (report)
Barnum, Betsy (correspondence)
Barsamian, David (interviewer)
   Excerpt from an interview with Noam Chomsky   (February, 1997)
Clark, Tony
   "By What Authority?" (International forum on   Globalization brochure)
Commonwealth of World Citizens
   "Who Speaks for Mankind?" (pamphlet)
Corporate Personhood Resolution of the City of Point Arena, California
The Council for Inter-American Security
   "The Santa Fe Report" (1980)
Eastman, Mary
   Poem inspired by the Minnesota state seal
Edwards, David
   "The Tale of Two 'Massacres' - Jenin and Racek" (Znet)
   Forum for Applied Research and Public Policy
   "Coming to Terms with Sustainability"
Holdridge, Sook
   "The Delusions We Have About Progress" (paper)
   "The Precautionary Principle" (paper)
Joiner, Max
   "Alliance for Democracy — MN Observations" (paper)
Kangas, Steve
   "The Origins of the Overclass" (paper)
   "A Timeline of CIA Atrocities" (paper)
Kehler, Randy
   *"Political Bribery in the U.S.A." (pamphlet)
Kennan, George
   "Policy Planning Study 23"
Kipling, Rudyard
   "The White Man's Burden" (poem)
MN Greens
   "The Ten Key Values of the Green Party"
Shove, David (correspondence)
Thompson, Sharon
   Assignment in "Active Nonviolence" class at   University of St. Thomas, St. Paul
United States Constitution
Wikipedia
Women's International League for Peace & freedom
   *Study guide "Challenge Corporate Power: Assert the People's Rights"

www.ingramcontent.com/pod-product-compliance
Lightning Source LLC
LaVergne TN
LVHW062318070526
838202LV00051B/4128